WRIGHT *of* DERBY

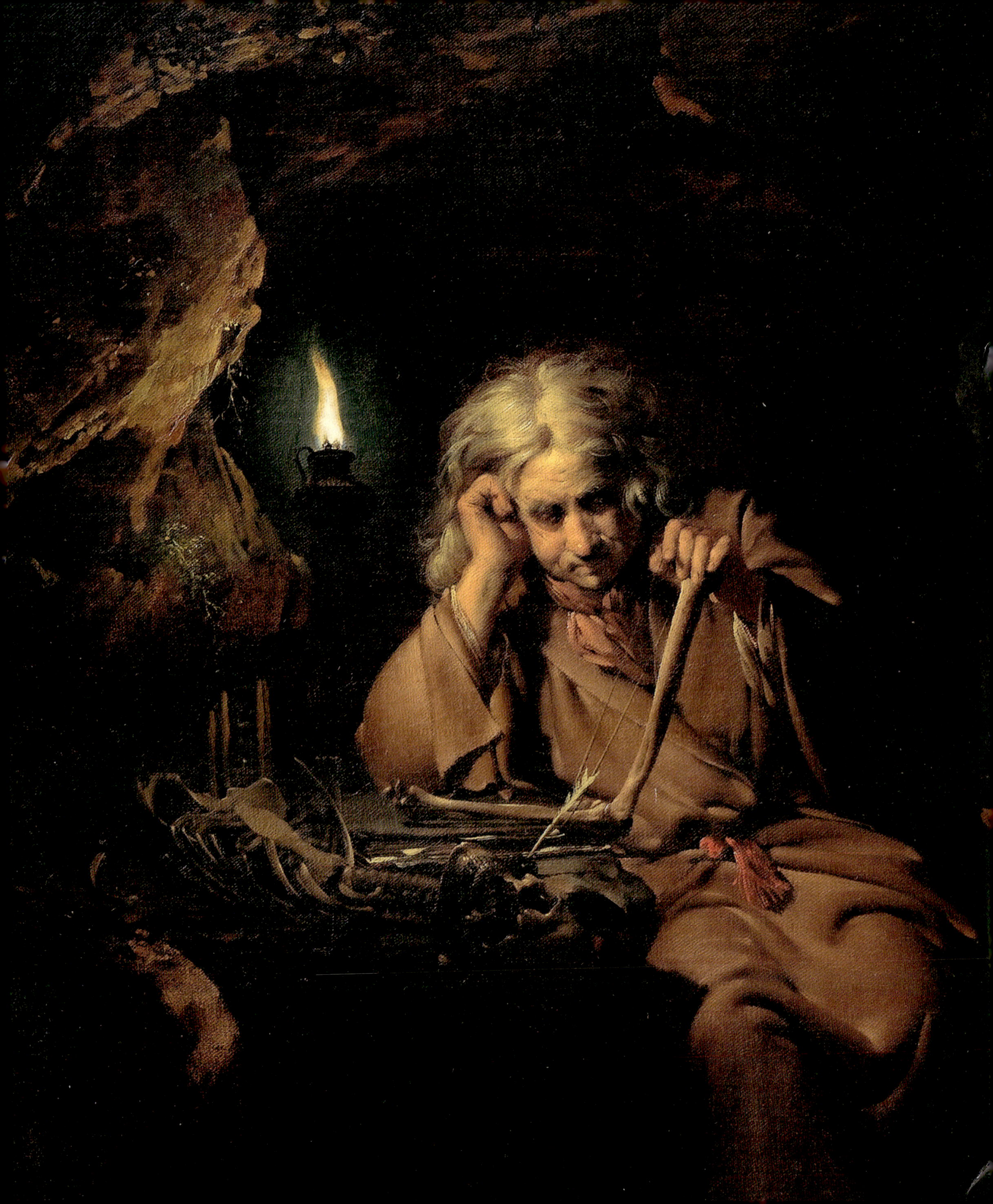

WRIGHT *of* DERBY

FROM THE SHADOWS

Christine Riding and Jon King

National Gallery Global, London
Distributed by Yale University Press

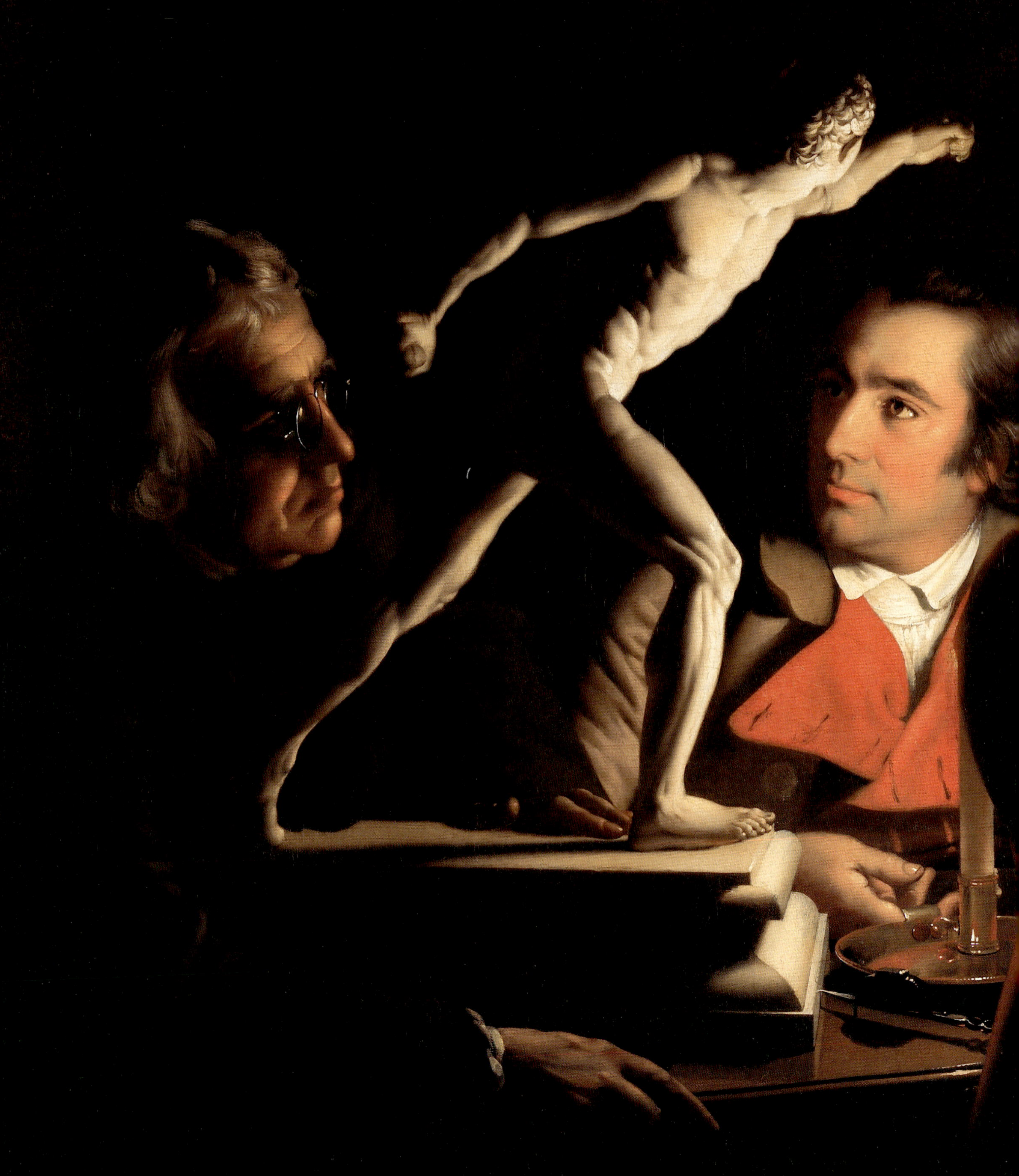

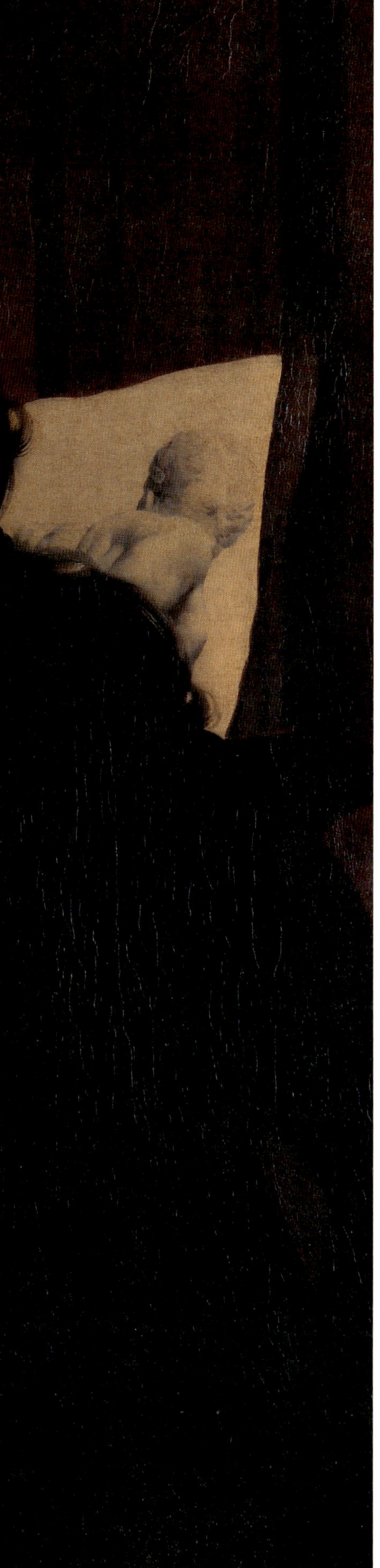

CONTENTS

DIRECTORS' FOREWORD

This exhibition is a collaborative endeavour between the Derby Museums and the National Gallery, and provides the occasion for Joseph Wright of Derby's two nocturnal masterpieces, *A Philosopher giving that Lecture on the Orrery in which a Lamp is put in the Place of the Sun* (1766) and *An Experiment on a Bird in the Air Pump* (1768), to be seen together by the public for the first time in 35 years. The scale and subject matter of these two paintings, the way in which they capture the Enlightenment's faith in scientific experimentation and observation, the skilful deployment of human emotions, their sapient allusions to the Baroque tradition of painted candlelight scenes, and their sheer technical brilliance help to explain why, over 250 years after they were made, they remain so compelling to modern audiences. With the aim of providing a context that deepens understanding of the artist's intentions, as well as the visual sources he drew on, the display brings together some thirty works from several different collections, and we wish to express our gratitude to all the lenders, both private and institutional.

Wright's nocturnes have recently been in the public eye, and they have also been the object of some fascinating scholarly research, notably Matthew Craske's 2020 volume *Joseph Wright of Derby: Painter of Darkness* and Julia Siemon's recent article in *The Burlington Magazine* (March 2025). A version of *Two Boys with a Bladder* was temporarily stopped from being exported from the United Kingdom in 2018, only to be acquired two years later by the Getty Museum in Los Angeles; a second version by the artist of the painting shown here, *An Academy by Lamplight*, was also stopped at export stage in 2020 and its present location remains unknown. Happily, though, Wright of Derby's painted study for *The Air Pump* (on the reverse of a superb self portrait), which documents his initial layout for part of the chiaroscuro scene, was acquired in 2022 by Derby Museums as a hybrid purchase and acceptance in lieu of tax, generously supported by donors including the National Heritage Memorial Fund.

We congratulate the exhibition curators, Christine Riding in London and Lucy Bamford in Derby. We would also like to thank Jon King for his involvement in shaping the exhibition and his insightful essay. At the National Gallery, we express our gratitude to The Thompson Family Charitable Trust for their generous grant to this exhibition and their continued support of the work of the Gallery. We would also like to thank our individual donors and the Bernard Sunley Foundation for their longstanding commitment to the Gallery through their invaluable support of the Sunley Room and its exhibitions programme.

For Derbeians, Wright is more than an artist. His work symbolises the spirit of experimentation and innovation that has characterised the city's 300-year history as a manufacturing centre ever since Derby Silk Mill (now the Museum of Making) was built in 1721. Today's technicians and engineers in Derby-based companies like Rolls-Royce, Alstom and Toyota trace a line to the climate of scientific endeavour of the Enlightenment. Derby Museums is delighted to share its stunning collections in the National Gallery while new light (pardon the pun) and understanding is shed on Wright's work. In turn, it is with great anticipation that *The Air Pump* will be shown in the Derby Museum and Art Gallery for the first time since the 1940s, when the exhibition comes to the city in 2026.

Sir Gabriele Finaldi
Director, The National Gallery, London

Tony Butler OBE
Executive Director, Derby Museums

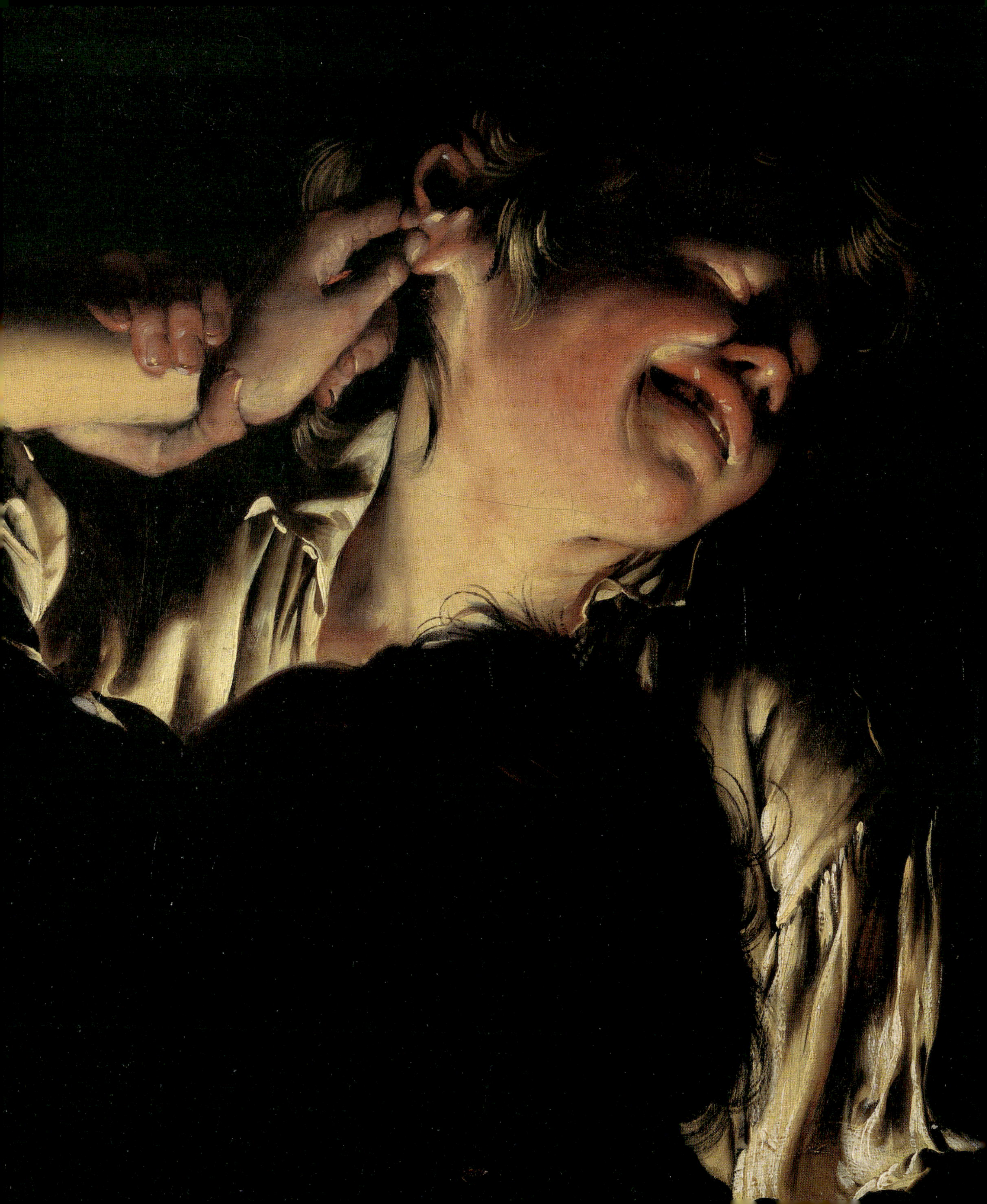

BETWEEN DARKNESS AND LIGHT

CHRISTINE RIDING

'ORRERY WRIGHT shall here the test abide,
In high historic stile, and epic pride...'
Anonymous, London, 1767[1]

In 1863, nearly a century after it was first exhibited, Edward Tyrrell gave *An Experiment on a Bird in the Air Pump* (pl. 6) by Joseph Wright of Derby to the National Gallery. Some twenty years later, in 1884, *A Philosopher giving that Lecture on the Orrery in which a Lamp is put in the Place of the Sun* (pl. 5) was purchased by public subscription and presented to the Derby Art Gallery. Since then, these publicly owned and permanently displayed paintings have become two of the most iconic images in the history of British art, not only for their imposing scale and visual power but also because they have – alongside the National Gallery's *The Fighting Temeraire* (1839) by J.M.W. Turner and *The Hay Wain* (1821) by John Constable – transcended the particular artistic moment that created them, to become symbolic of an entire period of British history, society and culture.[2]

While Wright could not have predicted what the future would hold for *The Air Pump* and *The Orrery*, there is little doubt that he was articulating in visual form matters of far broader interest, meaning and concern than those of the mid-Georgian art market. But subsequent references to him being an artist 'of the Enlightenment' or 'of the Industrial Revolution' – partly in response to the scientific themes of the two paintings, Wright's acquaintance with members of the Lunar Society of Birmingham, and later representations associated with the industrialist Richard Arkwright – would, in reality, have had little meaning for the artist and his contemporaries,

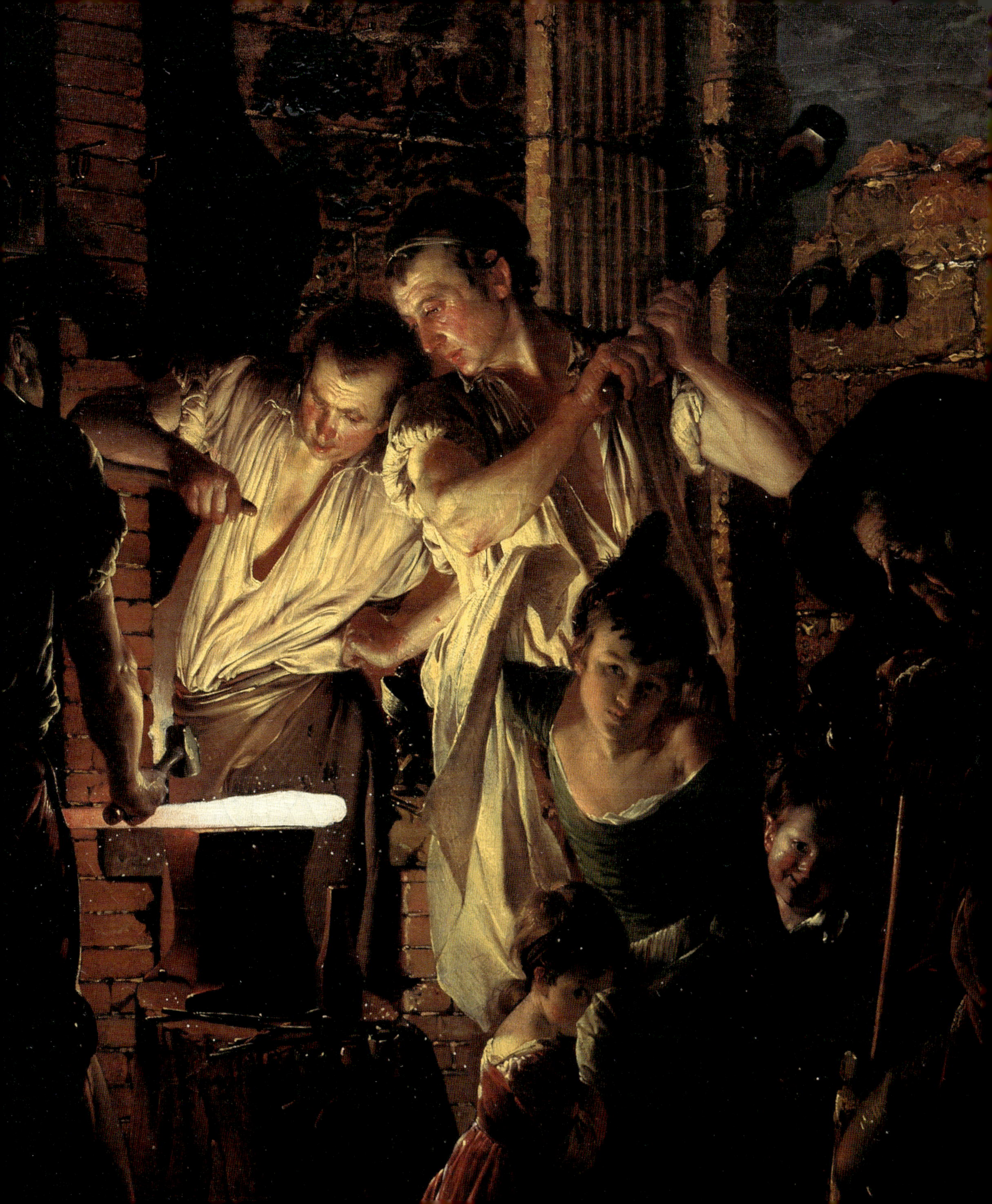

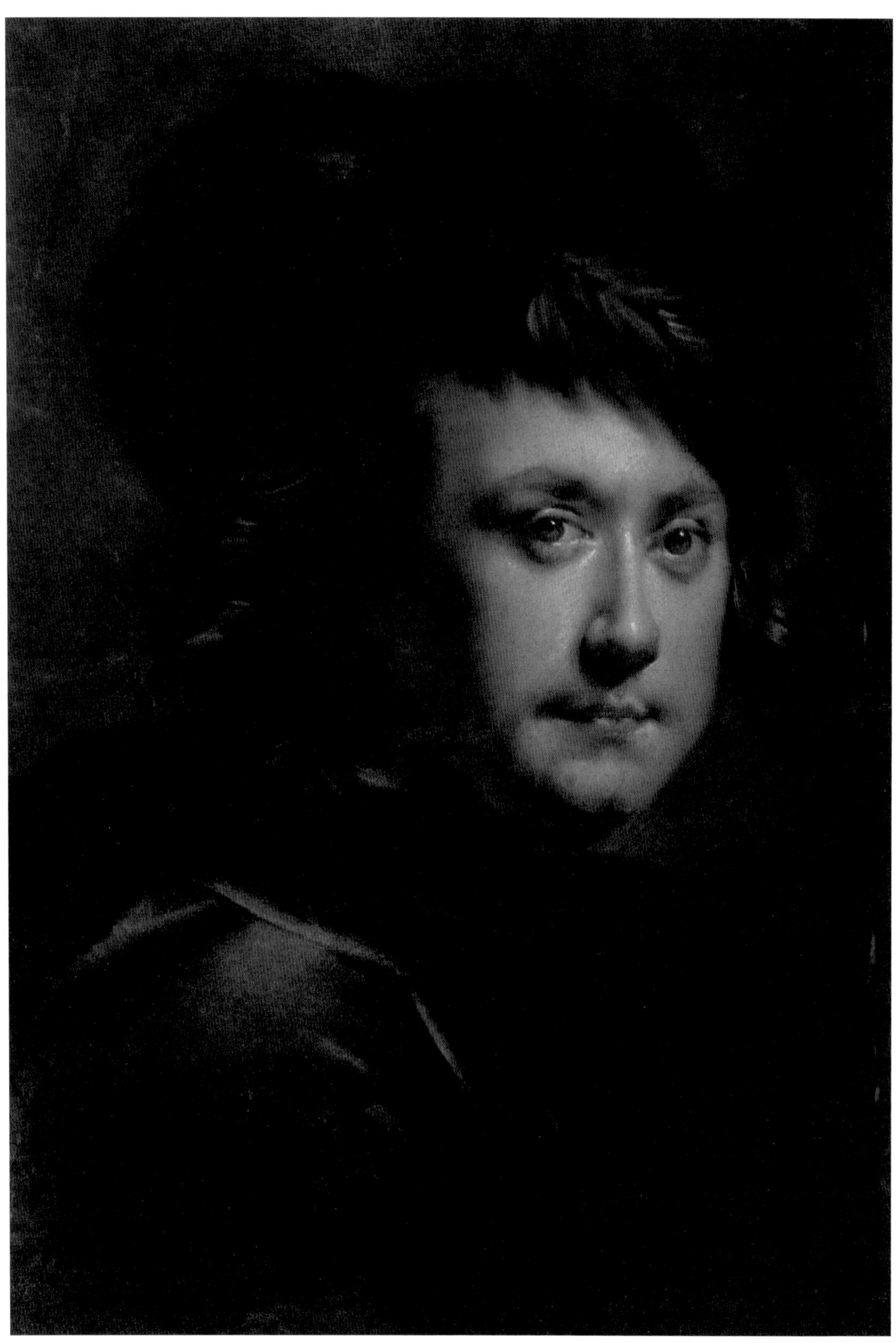

not least because both terms, 'Enlightenment' and 'Industrial Revolution', were first coined in Britain in the late nineteenth century.[3] In his own estimation, Wright was first and foremost a painter, who, over a career lasting some forty years, engaged with a wide range of artistic genres, interests, styles and associations: from portraits and landscapes, through modern and classical literature and history, to contemporary events and trends (fig. 1). However, it was with his depictions centring on the dramatic effects of light and darkness, referred to at the time as 'candlelights' (or 'night pieces'), which he deployed for numerous subjects, in different types of composition, and on various scales – scenes of art connoisseurship and schooling, scientific demonstrations and discoveries, childhood play and conflict, working-class labour and philosophical enquiry – that Wright was able to distinguish himself from his peers and to gain long-lasting renown.[4]

Initially, this acclaim was due to Wright's distinctive use of tenebrism (from the Italian word 'tenebroso', meaning 'darkened' or 'obscured') – a style of painting associated with the late work of the Baroque artist Caravaggio and his many followers in Italy and Northern Europe, including Orazio and Artemisia Gentileschi, Bartolomeo Manfredi, Hendrick ter Brugghen, Gerrit van Honthorst, Adam de Coster and Jusepe de Ribera.[5] This style was characterised by an unprecedented level of realism combined with an extreme form of chiaroscuro (meaning 'light and dark'), itself a feature of Western painting since the High Renaissance. However, rather than merely assisting in the illusion of three-dimensional forms and spaces, tenebrism made darkness a central component of the picture. As discussed below, Caravaggio's innovative approach had the effect of imbuing even the most ordinary scenes and subjects with the kind of visual and psychological power that was associated during Wright's lifetime with the 'sublime'.[6]

Importantly for Wright, it was also a tradition increasingly admired by international collectors and connoisseurs, but with few precedents, champions or practitioners in eighteenth-century British art. By 1770, the claustrophobic intensity of Wright's earliest candlelight paintings would transition into a series of night scenes, where exterior and interior spaces were contrasted by natural (moonlight) and artificial light (from lanterns, smithies and iron forges), respectively, and where the European landscape tradition, as represented by the Neapolitan Salvator Rosa, and Wright's near contemporaries Richard Wilson and Claude-Joseph Vernet, was a key inspiration.[7] But his fascination with the artistic possibilities of darkness and light remained a constant.

The purpose of the present publication is, therefore, to explore this specific aspect of Wright's early to mid-career, embracing the period from 1765, when he began exhibiting in London, to 1773 when he travelled to Italy to further his professional goals, after which his focus and style shifted significantly towards pure landscapes and poignant or poetic narratives drawn from literature (see pl. 27). Between these two auspicious dates, Wright established himself as one of the most exciting and innovative artistic talents working in Britain, who by the early 1770s had achieved an international reputation through the public display and sale of his candlelight paintings, and (just as importantly) their dissemination in Britain and beyond via reproduction as luxury mezzotints (see pp. 55–7). In so doing, Wright was actively engaging with and contributing to a period of profound change in British visual arts, resulting in the social as well as cultural elevation of the artist.[8] Indeed, his mastery of the candlelight format meant that he was able to simultaneously energise a seventeenth-century tradition firmly ascribed to the old masters, while broadening its

Fig. 1 *Self Portrait in a Black Feathered Hat*, about 1770–3, pastel on blue paper, 53.3 × 36.8 cm, Derby Museums

appeal beyond the exclusive world of art patrons and connoisseurs, in part because much of his subject matter was so contemporary and therefore relatable.

THE MAKING OF 'ORRERY WRIGHT'

When focusing on his candlelight and night scenes, it should be remembered that Wright launched his career in the mid-1750s as a provincial portrait painter, at a time when portraiture dominated British art production. European artists had long been encouraged through their training and practice to draw on the lessons of the past by closely observing the styles of classical Greek and Roman sculpture and Italian Renaissance painters, particularly Raphael, Michelangelo and Titian. Without significant state patronage for the arts or an academy along the formal lines common on the Continent, however, British-born artists were perceived to be at a disadvantage – above all when it came to history painting, then understood to be the most formally and intellectually demanding of all genres of art, and thus the most prestigious.[9]

What compounded the situation was the 'classical' bias of aristocratic culture in Britain, exemplified by the eighteenth-century phenomenon known as the Grand Tour, which took the sons of the nobility and landed gentry on excursions across Europe to Italy, with extended stays in Rome and its environs. One of the main drivers of such a tour was art appreciation and taste-making, which profoundly affected attitudes to collecting and commissioning paintings, with patrons intent on acquiring – while abroad and after their return – examples by Italian Renaissance masters, Baroque artists including Salvator Rosa, and such revered seventeenth-century French classicists as Claude Lorrain and Nicolas Poussin. Their paintings, incorporating mythological and biblical themes and narratives, set a standard in history painting and the associated genre of historical landscape that British artists were thought technically and intellectually incapable of emulating.[10]

This long-held bias meant that British artists were also competing for patronage against leading contemporary Italian or Rome-based artists such as Canaletto, Claude-Joseph Vernet and Pompeo Girolamo Batoni, the latter the principal portraitist in Rome for visitors from abroad.[11] Batoni's Grand Tour portrait *par excellence* of Sir Wyndham Knatchbull-Wyndham shows precisely what Wright and fellow British artists were up against, even in the realm of portraiture (fig. 2). Posing within a classical interior, the young aristocrat gestures towards a temple beyond, his flamboyant Van Dyck costume, far from being mere 'fancy dress', here pointing unequivocally to the cultural authority of King Charles I and the Stuart court, via whom the notion of the Grand Tour itself had developed.[12] Hence Wright's determination to travel to Rome in 1773 – as noted by his niece and early biographer, Hannah – reflected the immense pressure felt by many in the cultural sphere at the time, succinctly expressed by the influential author and lexicographer Dr Samuel Johnson only three years after Wright's departure: 'Sir, a man who has not been in Italy is always conscious of an inferiority, from his not having seen what it is expected a man should see.'[13]

On one level, then, the challenge for Wright and his fellow painters (whether they had been to Italy or not) was to attract Grand Tourists and other wealthy clients, while simultaneously raising contemporary British art in their estimation. This may in part explain Wright's

Fig. 2 Pompeo Girolamo Batoni, *Portrait of Sir Wyndham Knatchbull-Wyndham*, about 1758, oil on canvas, 233.1 × 161.3 cm, Los Angeles County Museum of Art

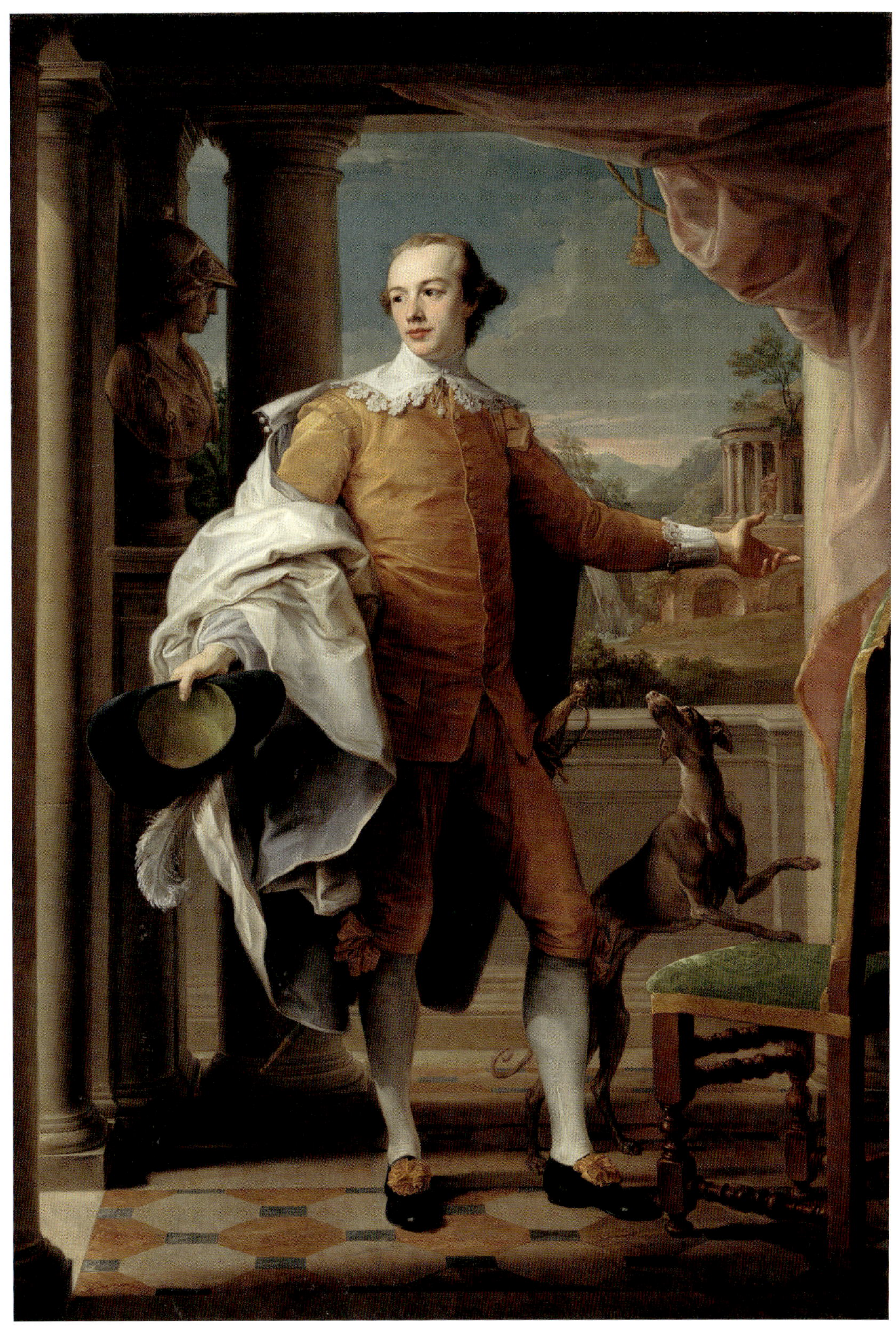

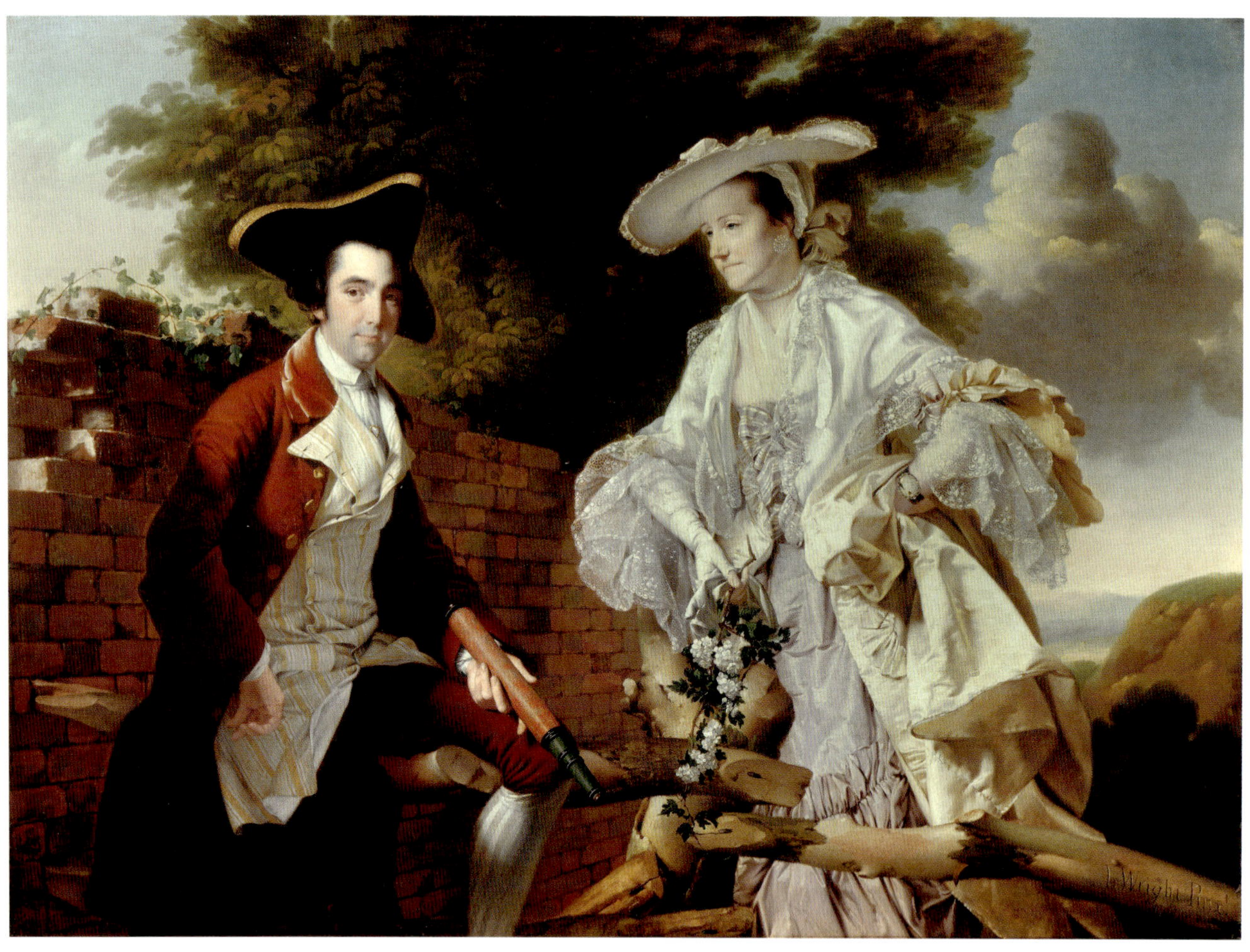

Fig. 3 *Portrait of Peter Perez Burdett and his First Wife Hannah*, 1765, oil on canvas, 145 × 205 cm, National Gallery, Prague

adoption of a seventeenth-century Continental tradition that originated in Rome and Naples, examples of which, whether by Caravaggio or the so-called 'Caravaggisti', would have been seen by travellers in Italy and elsewhere in Europe, and were present in private collections in the UK.[14] Out of commercial necessity, portraiture would remain a major strand for Wright, both as a vital source of income and as a means of networking, with portraits amounting to more than half of his entire output.[15] However, Wright was a serious-minded individual with higher aspirations. He concluded, as did many of his generation, that to raise his professional standing he needed to broaden his range into other genres, while engaging strategically with the opportunities presented by the rapidly evolving London art world, despite being the first major British painter to work almost entirely outside the capital.[16] Wright's life-long objective was to succeed as both a provincial and a cosmopolitan artist.

Referred to as 'of Derby' (his birthplace) from early on in his career, initially perhaps to distinguish him from another painter with the same surname, Wright seems to have viewed this melding of person and place as commercially advantageous (by being distinctive from those artists based in London). With a local client base for portraiture comprising members of the aristocracy, landed gentry and professional classes, he may also have deemed it financially astute, given the considerable expense of a studio-house in the capital. Furthermore, his roots in the English Midlands – Joseph was the third of five children of Hannah Brookes and John Wright, an attorney and the town clerk of Derby, a thriving market town – ran much deeper than providing a source of income and inspiration: they were central to his personal identity and regional loyalties and friendships.[17] In fact, it was through such connections that Wright received encouragement as well as commissions for his subject paintings, including *The Orrery* and *The Air Pump*.

Even so, London in the 1750s and 1760s was vital to Wright's development and success; and it was where he trained to be an artist. Starting at the age of 17, he spent two periods (1751–3 and 1756–7) in the studio of the prominent and well-connected portrait painter Thomas Hudson, whose pupil a decade earlier had been Joshua Reynolds. Wright's training included studying casts of classical sculpture, old master prints and drawings in Hudson's personal collection, and then drapery and poses from the elder artist's portraits.[18] Wright's technique and handling during the 1760s, utilising close and evenly applied brushstrokes to create a smooth and highly polished finish, were developed from Hudson's example. His growing confidence in applying these formal qualities to increasingly complex, large-scale compositions is evident in the spectacular double portrait of his friend, cartographer and engraver Peter Perez Burdett and his first wife, Hannah (fig. 3). This clear, sharp-edged and boldly coloured technique was also well suited to the dramatic effects he sought to create in his early candlelight paintings and was deployed in a similarly individualistic manner by George Stubbs, a self-taught artist born in Liverpool who moved to London in 1759, and Johann Zoffany, from near Frankfurt, who arrived the following year. Significantly, perhaps, it was also characteristic of Batoni's cosmopolitan style, drawn from Italian Renaissance art and French and Bolognese classicism, among other influences.[19]

Over and above what he would have learned and observed directly from Thomas Hudson during the 1750s, Wright was living in the heart of the city's vibrant contemporary art world, centred around Leicester Fields (now Leicester Square), nearby Covent Garden and, to the north, Lincoln's Inn Fields, where Hudson was based. Wright would, therefore, have taken advantage of, and been stimulated by, the shared aims, ambitions and spirit of cooperation between the artists associated with the St Martin's Lane Academy, established in 1735 under the leadership of William Hogarth, and the public art projects they generated.[20] Zoffany painted the only known representation of a life class at the Academy (1761–2, Royal Academy Collection), which continued to operate until 1767, showing the attendees drawing and discussing their work by lamplight, then standard practice across Europe, with casts of antique busts and framed chalk drawings displayed at the back of the room. The subject of study and drawing – whether for professional or amateur purposes – was itself an established and resonant theme in British art, and accordingly featured in Wright's early portraits of the young brothers Samuel and William Rastall (about 1762–4, private collection) and in two of his candlelight subjects, *Three Persons viewing the Gladiator by Candlelight* (pl. 1), and the two versions of *An Academy by Lamplight* (see fig. 25 and pl. 2), which he painted while resident in Liverpool from late 1768 to 1771.

TRANSFORMING BRITISH ART

Alongside art tutelage and drawing academies, there were other initiatives in London that specifically aimed to promote a modern school of British art to a broader audience and would have caught any aspiring artist's eye. For example, at Vauxhall Pleasure Gardens, the fashionable Thames-side entertainment resort, among the main attractions from the 1740s were the supper boxes and pavilions decorated with paintings by Francis Hayman and his assistants.[21] At the same time, the Foundling Hospital (established in 1739) hosted the first artistic scheme of its kind in the country, launched just four years before Wright's arrival in London. History paintings, portraiture, topographical views and other genres – by Hogarth, Hayman, Hudson and other leading figures like Joseph Highmore and Allan Ramsay, alongside younger talents including Reynolds and Thomas Gainsborough – were assembled to form an impressive and varied collection of British art for visitors to peruse in the public rooms.[22] One painting that undoubtedly interested Wright personally and professionally was Hogarth's *March of the Guards to Finchley* (fig. 4), acquired by the hospital in 1750. It shows British soldiers marshalling in 1745 to defend London from the Jacobite army led by Charles Edward Stuart ('Bonnie Prince Charlie') as it marched south from Edinburgh, through England, as far as Derby. The 11-year-old Joseph Wright and his siblings had been evacuated in haste to nearby Repton, as the family home in the centre of Derby was used temporarily as a billet by occupying officers and soldiers.[23] Hogarth's painting – part factual, part allegory – was also more than a hint to Wright as to how a familiar or newsworthy subject that chimed with the lived experience of contemporary viewers (as seen, for example, in *The Orrery* and *The Air Pump*) could be transformed via the ingenuity of an ambitious artist into the realms of high art.[24]

Following on from such groundbreaking artistic programmes at urban venues, the 1760s saw a significant turning point in the creation and public display of contemporary art, with the growth of a dynamic exhibition culture alongside an already buoyant print market. This was signalled by the founding of a succession of improving societies, starting with the Edinburgh Society for Encouraging Arts, Sciences, Manufactures and Agriculture in Scotland (a subsidiary of the Select Society) in 1755, followed four years later by London's Society for the Encouragement of the Arts, Manufactures and Commerce (Society of Arts) and its offshoots, the Society of Artists of Great Britain (1761) and the Free Society of Artists (1762), leading ultimately to the formation of the Royal Academy of Arts in 1768. Comparable initiatives beyond London included Liverpool's Society of Artists, formed in 1769 by none

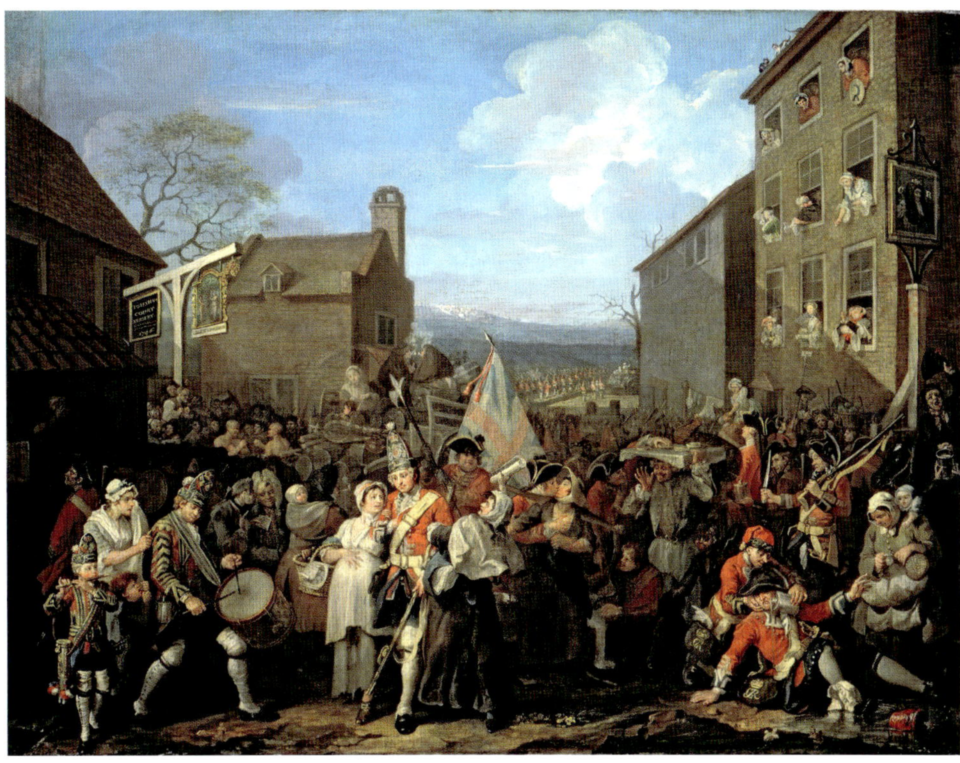

Fig. 4 William Hogarth, *The March of the Guards to Finchley*, 1750, oil on canvas, 100.3 × 133.3 cm, Foundling Museum, London

other than Peter Perez Burdett, who became its first president.[25] In fact, the idea for annual exhibitions in London had been proposed publicly as early as 1754 and these were then inaugurated in 1760, under the auspices of the Society of Arts, which also initiated an annual prize to promote history painting based on British historical and literary subjects.[26] Wright exhibited almost exclusively at the Society of Artists until 1778, despite the Royal Academy having swiftly established itself as the premier contemporary art forum and school in Britain under the presidency of Joshua Reynolds.[27]

The history of public exhibiting in London is complicated and was not without controversy at the time (see p. 49).[28] Nevertheless, the existence of multiple (albeit competing) societies and exhibition venues meant that artists had the opportunity to play an increasingly prominent role in British public life, with audiences for their work expanding far beyond the exclusive world of connoisseurs, patrons and critics. Now art was seen by anyone who had the inclination and could afford the entrance ticket. Some were there to view the latest examples of British art, a few were there to purchase, many more to experience or be part of a spectacle. One can appreciate the likely appeal of Wright's *Gladiator*, *Orrery* and *Air Pump* to a wide range of exhibition visitors, not least in seeing themselves 'reflected', so to speak, in such eye-catching pictures. Unsurprisingly, this novel turn of events was favoured by young and provincial artists – Wright was both in 1760 – seeking success and recognition in the capital. In order to stand out among their fellows and competitors, many artists developed their styles, subjects and compositions accordingly to gain a visual and therefore critical advantage. Importantly for the progress of Wright's career, this exhibiting culture encouraged the more pioneering artists to adopt or promote a 'signature' style.[29]

Assuming that Wright was keeping an eye on trends and innovations on view in London from the early 1760s, he would have noted that his contemporaries Wilson, Gainsborough, Reynolds and Stubbs were already using the context of public display to experiment, testing the market (as Wright would do) for painting categories other than society portraiture – landscape, fancy pictures, history and genre – with compositions that were just as ambitious and steeped in the old master tradition, yet were unconventional and/or still to achieve any significant traction with British art patrons. And it is in this context, as an exhibitor, that Wright's identification with the candlelight tradition should be

Fig. 5 Joshua Reynolds, *Garrick between Tragedy and Comedy*, 1761, oil on canvas, 183 × 147.6 cm, Waddesdon Manor

Fig. 6 George Stubbs, *Horse devoured by a Lion*, exhibited 1763, oil on canvas, 69.2 × 103.5 cm, Tate, London

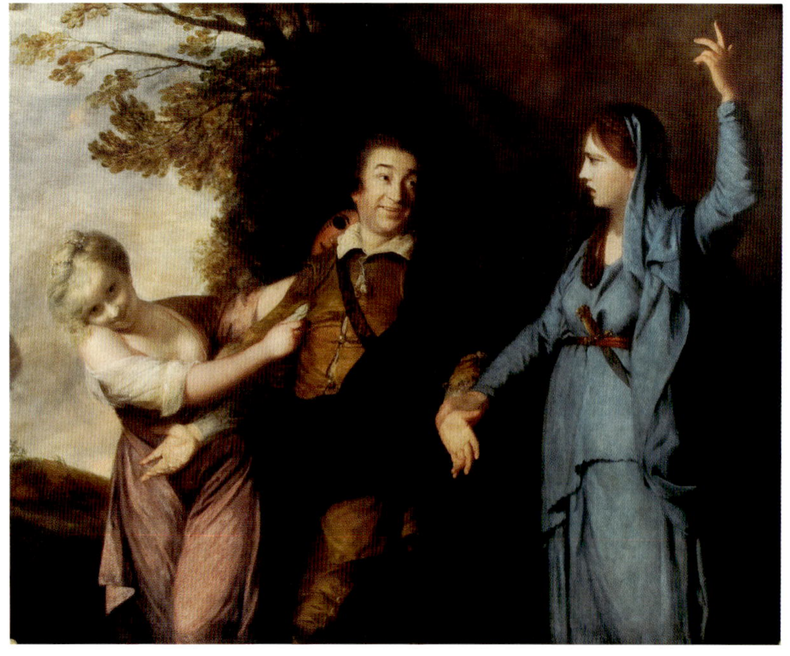

viewed. For example, at the very first London exhibition in 1760, Richard Wilson caused a sensation with *The Destruction of the Children of Niobe* (see fig. 15). Here was a British artist mastering the hybrid style of mythological narrative in a landscape setting, brought to prominence by Claude, but in this instance taking inspiration from the wild, untamed compositions of Salvator Rosa. Equally instructive for Wright was that an engraving after *Niobe* was published the following year and proved so popular that it spurred commissions for Wilson to repeat the subject for other patrons.[30]

Wright's interest in the landscapes of Rosa and Wilson would surface a decade later in two night scenes displayed in 1773, *An Iron Forge viewed from Without* (see fig. 14) and *An Earthstopper on the Banks of the Derwent* (pl. 14), underlining a marked shift in subject – particularly the focus on working-class labour – and composition from his earliest exhibits. The point being made here is that artists were emboldened by the tactics and successes of their peers. Thus, on a speculative basis, Gainsborough began submitting ambitious large-scale landscapes – melding Claudean idealism with seventeenth-century Dutch naturalism – to the Society of Artists in 1763, alongside his portraits, for which there was a more established and lucrative market.[31] At the same time, Reynolds took a particularly innovative approach to his unique brand of Grand Manner portraiture, incorporating classical and Renaissance ideals (developed after his return from Italy in 1752), when he exhibited his large-scale *Garrick between Tragedy and Comedy* (fig. 5) in 1762; while overtly allegorising a contemporary person, in this case the pioneering actor

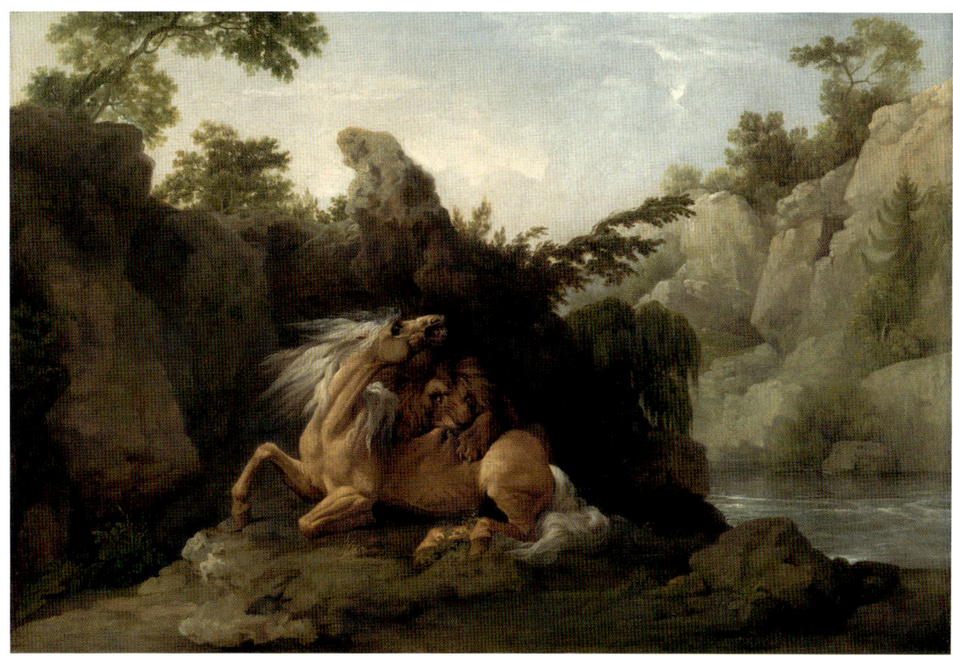

and theatre impresario David Garrick, Reynolds also signalled how artists could now trade on the celebrity (and notoriety) of performers and other public figures to engage and entertain visitors.[32]

Similarly, in submitting *Horse frightened by a Lion* and its companion *Horse devoured by a Lion* (fig. 6) to the Society of Artists in 1763, Stubbs established his intellectual credentials and first-hand experience of Italy by choosing a subject that had its antecedence in the classical sculpture he had studied at the Palazzo dei Conservatori in Rome.[33] However, he made the subject his own by setting the scene in a British rather than Italianate/idealised landscape – Creswell Crags near the Peak District – while also delineating with astonishing anatomical accuracy the terror and violence of the encounter, hence capitalising on its emotional and narrative power. Skilfully encapsulating the formalities of history painting, Stubbs elevated himself and his art beyond the highly commercial but less critically regarded genres of sporting art and equine portraiture, examples of which he had also submitted to the exhibition.[34]

BRITAIN'S CARAVAGGIO?

It was in this rich and competitive environment that Wright made his London debut at the Society of Artists in 1765, as both a portraitist and subject painter, with two works of art, the aforementioned *Three Persons viewing the Gladiator by Candlelight* and an unidentified portrait, described in the exhibition catalogue as 'a conversation' and possibly that of his friend Burdett and his wife (see fig. 3).[35] Wright rarely (if ever) adopted a 'tenebrist' effect in his portraiture, except revealingly in some of his self portraits (see fig. 1). Hence the striking contrast between *The Gladiator* and a portrait such as that of the Burdetts (his largest and most ambitious at that date) may well have been a determining factor in Wright's choice of submissions, by highlighting his range and technical versatility, including, within *The Gladiator*, the painted representation of drawing and sculpture media.[36] Here the context of display is crucial – that is, the densely hung, public exhibitions where his paintings would attract, if not demand, attention. The subject and treatment of *The Gladiator* were also calculated to appeal to art patrons and connoisseurs by showing three men absorbedly studying a copy of the *Borghese Gladiator*, one of the most admired from antiquity (see p. 42). The life-size original (now in the Musée du Louvre) was then in the Villa Borghese in Rome and consequently familiar to Grand Tourists, with numerous versions on various scales in British collections (see pl. 3), including the celebrated bronze cast (now at Windsor Castle) made by Hubert Le Sueur for Charles I.[37]

In terms of his candlelight paintings more broadly, the lesson that Wright evidently drew from his fellow artists was that adopting the style and subject matter of an admired European tradition was not enough to engage an increasingly diverse art-interested public: one needed to both embrace it and then reinvent it for a contemporary British audience. Given the importance of a signature style, the novelty of Wright's tenebrist treatment, in British art at least, was as important as his choice of subjects. Compare, for example, Wright's *Gladiator* or (more directly) *An Academy by Lamplight* with a painting on a similar theme and scale, *A Conversation (The Artist's Brothers Peter and James Romney)* by George Romney (fig. 7), which was exhibited at the Free Society of Artists in 1766.[38] In the case of Wright's *Orrery* and *Air Pump*, the subjects and associated compositions were unprecedented in British art. Wright's first known painting in this vein, *A Girl reading a Letter by Candlelight* (private collection), dates to the early 1760s, at about the same time as Romney executed three small-scale candlelights, including one featuring his brother James, dated 1761 (Abbot Hall Art Gallery).[39] Unlike Wright, Romney did not pursue this style of painting further, but it is possible that both young artists were responding at the time to similar market trends and source material.

One such historical influence may have been the Dutch genre painter and portraitist Godfried Schalcken (see also p. 36 and fig. 19), who worked in London between 1692 and 1697, and whose candlelight paintings, including *Boy blowing on a Firebrand to light a Candle* (about 1692–8, National Gallery of Scotland), were already represented in British private collections.[40] Schalcken trained with Gerrit Dou, one of Rembrandt's most celebrated pupils, who specialised in the kind of exquisitely detailed, small-scale candlelit scenes that find parallels with Wright's *An Academy by Lamplight*, as well as *A Philosopher by Lamplight* (pl. 11) and *The Alchymist* (pl. 12), the latter two exhibited in 1769 and 1771, respectively.[41] More current exemplars were a group of mezzotints by the Irish artist Thomas Frye, representing life-size 'fanciful heads' (see fig. 29) arranged in diverse poses under candlelight conditions, which were published in London between 1760 and 1762 (one was exhibited at the Society of Arts in 1760) and have long been associated with specific figures seen in Wright's *Air Pump* and *An Academy by Lamplight* (see p. 56).[42]

Of course, Wright trained as a figurative artist and was able to transfer the subtlety of expression, gesture and pose that stemmed from his burgeoning portrait practice to his candlelight paintings, and vice versa. But the opportunities presented by tenebrism must have been additionally striking to Wright: the style alone could evoke a mood or emotion, not just visible actions but states of mind. In the Caravaggesque tradition, this was achieved compositionally by placing the human figures – sometimes half or three-quarter length, and habitually on the scale of life – up against the picture plane, giving them an immediacy for the viewer standing before the canvas. The intensity of the scene was enhanced by the illusion of a single, directed light source, often set against impenetrable darkness, so concentrating attention on the expressions and gestures of the protagonists. This also tested the artist's ability to evoke different textures and surfaces – skin, textiles, metals and so on – under such

Fig. 7 George Romney, *A Conversation (The Artist's Brothers Peter and James Romney)*, 1766, oil on canvas, 110.5 × 87.6 cm, Yale Center for British Art, Paul Mellon Collection

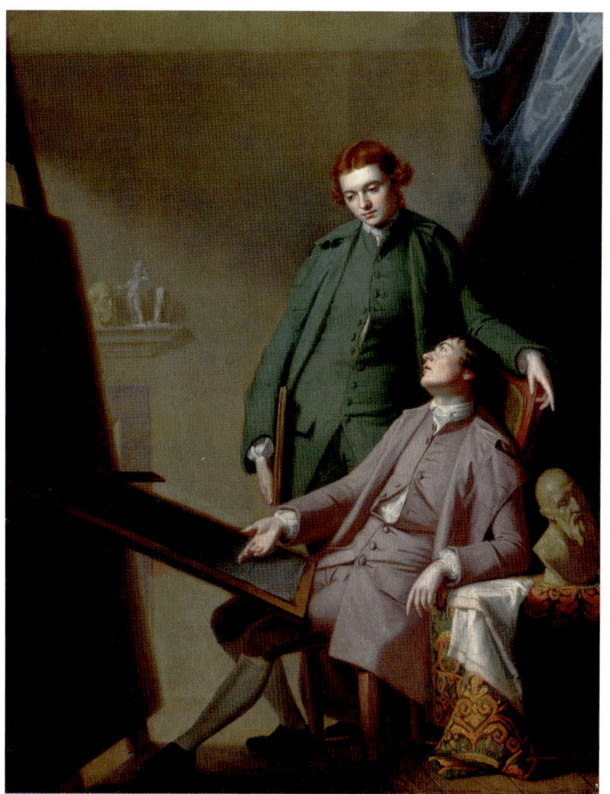

conditions, and equally to note how the perception of colour alters.[43] While Wright would have studied closely any available paintings and engravings to attempt to understand how such an effect was achieved in the past, on a practical level he had to come to his own conclusions through extensive observations and experiments.

Over and above the standard practice of drawing by lamplight (see p. 16), one method Wright deployed (according to his niece Hannah) involved two rooms in his brother Richard's house, one in darkness arranged with objects, and one lit from which he could observe how light and shadow behaved: some years later, he continued to experiment, using a box-like contraption of his own invention (see p. 36).[44] Wright likewise varied his technique: adjusting his mixture of pigments and layering of oil paint to achieve different effects from picture to picture.[45] More intriguingly, he also used metal leaf more extensively than was previously supposed, specifically beneath paint layers of the areas in and around the 'source' of light.[46] During recent technical analysis of *The Air Pump*, for instance, silver leaf was discovered within the area of candlelight diffused through the large rounded glass containing a diseased human skull.[47] This unconventional use of precious metal likely sprang from Wright observing its highly visible reflectivity, with silver

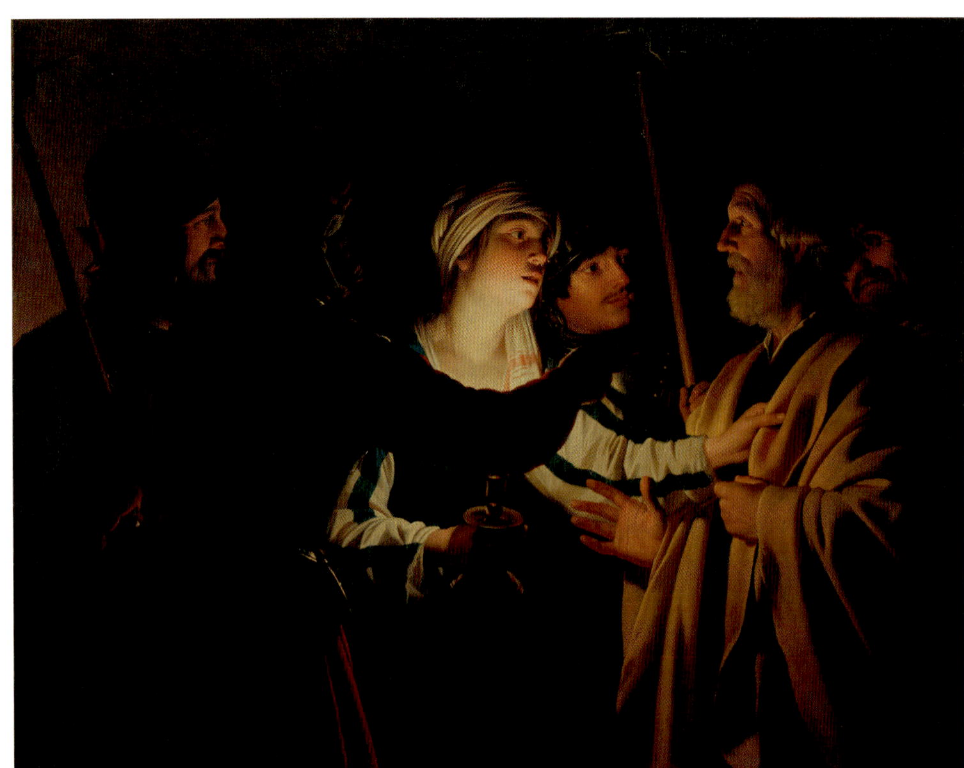

(the most reflective of all metals) commonly deployed in mirror making and for lighting such as candelabra and sconces. This technique was clearly meant to enhance the intensity of light from candles, lamps or heated metals.[48] More straightforwardly, Wright would also have noted how versatile the tenebrist or candlelight approach was during the seventeenth century: it was applied to contemporary subjects, settings and models, as well as historical or fictional narratives, and it embraced various categories of art, from history painting to genre painting (scenes of everyday life), and from complex group compositions to single figures or pairs of figures.[49]

Between 1765 and 1768 inclusively, Wright exhibited seven candlelight paintings that, broadly speaking, fall into two distinct formats within the tenebrist/candlelight tradition.[50] Exemplars, on religious and secular themes respectively, are *The Denial of Saint Peter* (fig. 8) by Gerrit (or Gerard) van Honthorst, and *A Man singing by Candlelight* (fig. 9) by Adam de Coster. Both artists were prominent 'Caravaggisti' and, interestingly, were known from the seventeenth century by the sobriquets 'Gherardo delle Notte' (Gerard of the Nights) and 'Pictor Noctium' (Painter of Nights).[51] Honthorst's painting is a large-scale crowd scene illustrating an episode from the Bible when a young maidservant accuses the apostle Peter (on the right) of knowing Jesus. Fearing for his own life, he denies the acquaintance and thus betrays his master. Both *The Orrery*, exhibited in 1766, and *The Air Pump*, shown in 1768, are comparable to this painting in terms of scale and formal complexity, and furthermore are likely meant to convey a similar aura of religiosity and/or moral profundity.

Hence Wright boldly elevates a self-evidently contemporary subject to the level conventionally reserved for history painting. In the picture by Coster, we see the type of secular genre scene that emerged during the seventeenth century, and for which Netherlandish artists were particularly renowned in Britain. As here, the candle flame itself is often blocked by a figure or an object (in this case, the musical score) – a striking pictorial device that Wright utilised, for example, in his *Gladiator*, *Orrery* and *Air Pump*, and even more markedly in *Two Boys fighting over a Bladder* (pl. 10).

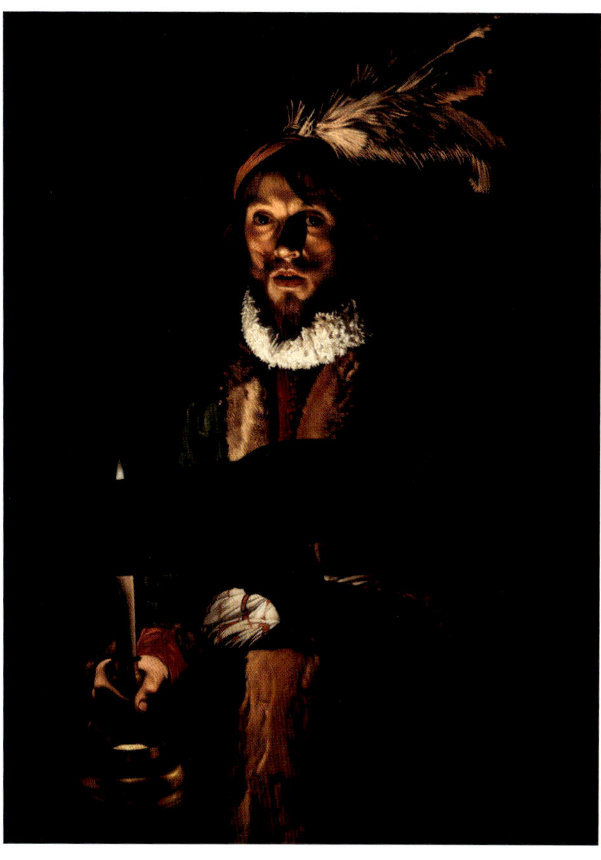

Fig. 8 Gerrit van Honthorst, *The Denial of Saint Peter*, about 1623, oil on canvas, 110.5 × 144.8 cm, Minneapolis Institute of Art

Fig. 9 Adam de Coster, *A Man singing by Candlelight*, between 1625 and 1635, oil on canvas, 123.6 × 90.7 cm, National Gallery of Ireland, Dublin

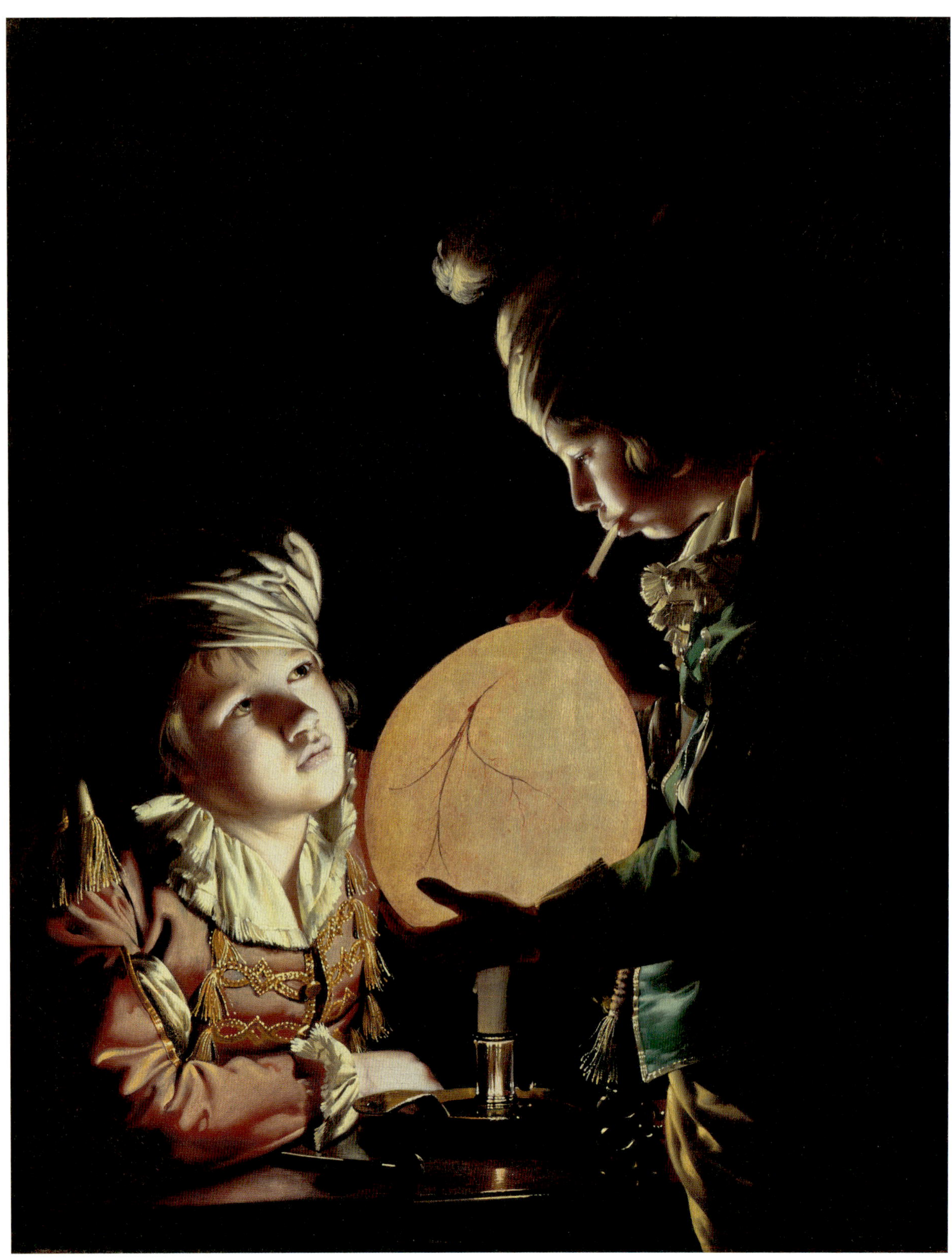

As we have seen, for some of Wright's candlelight paintings, the subjects were not new to European art. This is particularly true of his genre paintings where, for example, children playing with bladders was an established theme in Dutch art, traditionally interpreted (alongside the representation of soap bubbles) as symbolising the emptiness of the material world or the fragility and brevity of life.[52] Wright returned to the subject of a girl reading by candlelight (pl. 9), also an established theme, but here he heightens the narrative tension by showing the second figure (her father or older husband?) intently looking over her shoulder, his left hand poised to snatch the letter, leaving us to wonder who has sent it. In the context of British art, these and two further images, *Two Girls dressing a Kitten by Candlelight* (see fig. 27) and its companion *Two Boys with a Bladder* (fig. 10), exhibited in 1767, come under the broader category of 'fancy pictures', which were paintings depicting everyday themes with elements of imagination, invention or storytelling. This was one of the most original and popular art forms, alongside 'conversation pieces' (see p. 28), to emerge in Britain in the 1720s and 1730s, influenced by the genre paintings of Philippe Mercier, Jean-Siméon Chardin and other contemporary French artists, who were in turn responding to Netherlandish traditions.[53] The term 'fancies' (then understood to mean 'fantasy') was first used in Britain in the late 1730s to describe Mercier's paintings of anonymous children and young female street vendors and domestic servants on the scale of life.[54] These were calculated primarily to be pleasurable to look at, in contrast to the more reflective and technically sophisticated imagery created by Chardin, such as *The Young Schoolmistress* (fig. 11), which was widely known in Britain through prints.[55]

Wright plays on the notion of fantasy through his conspicuous use of elaborate costume or 'fancy dress' in his two small-scale paintings of 1767, which he repeated in *An Academy by Lamplight*. But, while portraying children (and adults) in costume was commonplace at this time, Wright's tenebrist treatment was not. In fact, on current evidence, the only British artist regularly exhibiting anything remotely comparable to Wright's candlelights was Henry Robert Morland, who, from 1764, showed a series of nocturnal 'fancies', which predominantly featured single female figures in the simplistic manner of Mercier, as well as lanterns, starting with *A Ballad Singer* (Yale Center for British Art).[56] Without serious competition, therefore, the field was left clear for Wright to take on the challenge of transforming the candlelight tradition for his own time. That he was

Fig. 10 *Two Boys with a Bladder*, 1767, oil on canvas, 92.7 × 73 cm, J. Paul Getty Museum, Los Angeles

Fig. 11 Jean-Siméon Chardin, *The Young Schoolmistress*, about 1737, oil on canvas, 61.6 × 66.7 cm, The National Gallery, London

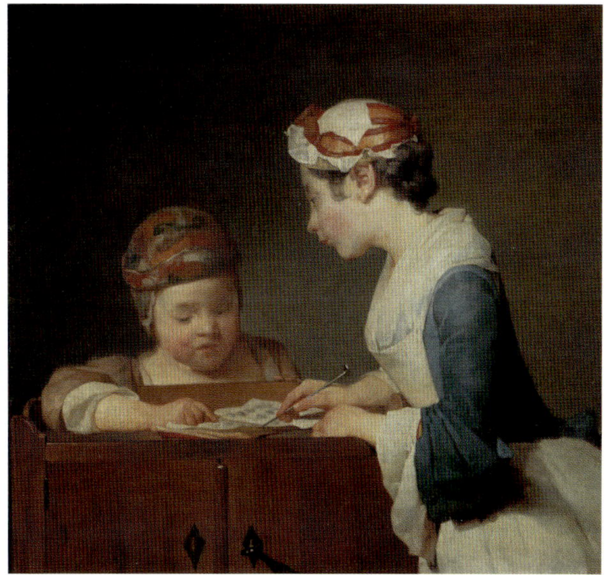

succeeding in the eyes of his contemporaries, even rivalling seventeenth-century masters, is made clear by the following published review of 1767: 'who, of all the Flemish and Dutch schools can equal Wright in still life? The magic of his light and shades is beyond description, his ideas how lovely, his execution how consummate!'[57]

LET THERE BE LIGHT

While seeking to make an impact on the art world via the candlelight tradition, Wright seems to have been genuinely fascinated by the relationship between light and its direct opposite, darkness. Of course, 'light' and 'dark' had powerful theological, intellectual and cultural connotations beyond art at the time, which would have been significant to Wright as a citizen, a Christian and an artist, and equally meaningful to the contemporary viewers of his paintings. In the book of Genesis, for example, the first act of creation springs from God's command 'Let there be light'. This signifies far more than the physical creation of light: it represents God's creative power and the establishment of order and time, of the celestial and terrestrial realms, contrasting with the initial state of formlessness and darkness.[58] Wright may have had such allusions in mind when conceiving his striking representations of 'god-like' lecturers in *The Air Pump* and *The Orrery* (see p. 44). Furthermore, in Christian theology Jesus is frequently described as 'the light', signifying his role as a source of spiritual enlightenment and guidance – a concept that features prominently in the Gospel of John, where Jesus declares, 'I am the light of the world: he that followeth me shall not walk in darkness, but shall have the light of life.'[59]

The juxtaposition of light and darkness also had a classical association with philosophy, going back to Plato's Allegory of the Cave (*Republic*, Book VII), which states that 'Light is knowledge of the true'.[60] Here 'the philosopher' is likened to a prisoner freed from a cave, who comes to understand that the shadows on its walls were not the direct reality of the objects within. Their true forms can only be viewed outside, in sunlight; that is, via the light of philosophical reason. The common ground linking such references is that prejudice and ignorance – associated with 'darkness' – have obscured our ability to perceive the truth. It is in this context that 'light' encapsulates the broad aims and values of 'the Enlightenment', as summarised visually by the now-famous frontispiece to Jean d'Alembert and Denis Diderot's *Encyclopédie*, published in Paris from 1751 to 1772, in which the female allegorical figure representing 'Truth', bathed in light, is unveiled by 'Reason' and 'Philosophy'.[61]

While 'Enlightenment' was not used in this context in English during Wright's lifetime, it evolved from two distinct eighteenth-century terms that were current in Britain: the French 'lumières' (meaning 'lights') and the German 'Aufklärung' (meaning a process of 'enlightenment').[62] This complex and (in the present) contested term describes the wide-reaching intellectual and philosophical movement in eighteenth-century Europe that emphasised reason and individualism, challenged traditional authority, and promoted ideas such as liberty, progress and tolerance.[63] A precondition to the Enlightenment was the so-called Scientific Revolution, a term that broadly covers the transformation during the sixteenth and seventeenth centuries of our understanding of the natural and physical worlds in several branches of what Wright and his contemporaries would have known as 'natural philosophy' and what we call 'the sciences' – astronomy, physics, chemistry and so on.[64] The English physicist and mathematician Sir Isaac Newton is seen as the culminating figure of the Scientific Revolution, whose discovery of the composition of white light integrated the phenomena of colours into the science of light. His three laws of motion – fundamental principles of modern physics – resulted in the formulation of the law of universal gravitation that provided an explanation for the orbits of the planets, and thus the groundwork for demonstrations such as the one we see in Wright's *Orrery*. Indeed, commentators have suggested that the central figure of the philosopher in the painting was meant to remind eighteenth-century viewers of the physical appearance of Newton.[65]

Such advances by Newton and others had set out that understanding stems from experience through experiment, not hypotheses. Integral to this paradigm shift was the invention and then improvement of scientific instruments such as telescopes, microscopes and air pumps (see pl. 8). The latter was invented in 1650, after which an improved version was developed and used by Robert Boyle and Dr Robert Hooke in 1659, to conduct groundbreaking experiments on the properties of air, including phenomena such as air pressure and the effects of air on respiration. Boyle and Hooke were also the first to experiment using birds and animals, placing sparrows, mice and kittens in the pump's receiver from which the air was removed.[66] The morality of this practice – where living creatures visibly convulsed and often died – was debated during the eighteenth century in the context of public demonstrations, when women and children were likely to be present. The Scottish astronomer and instrument maker James Ferguson went further by stating that such experiments were 'too shocking to every spectator who has the least degree of humanity'.[67] Hence the contemporary resonance of the 'life or death' moment represented in Wright's *Air Pump*.

Such instruments and demonstration devices were often valued for practical and aesthetic reasons, with the makers, some of whom were members of the prestigious Royal Society, being both engineers and craftsmen. This is particularly true of the orrery, the first of which was made in 1704 by clockmakers George Graham and Thomas Tompion. Later, John Rowley made one and named it after his patron, Charles Boyle, 4th Earl of Orrery, who was a relative of Robert Boyle.[68] An orrery is a moving model of the solar system, an improvement on the traditional static planetarium. Orreries varied in scale and could be portable or table-based, typically driven by a clockwork mechanism. The sun is represented by a globe at the centre, with a planet or a moon at the end of a series of metal arms that determine their relative positions and orbits. Wright's painting shows a 'grand orrery' (because it includes the outer planets then known) and, in addition, the skeletal framework of metal bands that were added to some of the most prestigious examples (see pl. 7). These represented the celestial sphere and were an integral part of an older astronomical instrument called an armillary sphere. Wright, who was fascinated by instruments in themselves, clearly saw the artistic – and specifically tenebrist – potential of a scene involving such a large, visually impressive orrery, with a group of people gathered around it.[69] Furthermore, the replacement of the sun's globe with a lamp, used to demonstrate solar and lunar phases and eclipses, only adds to the complex interplay between light and dark in the painting, with the metal bands casting additional shadows on the man taking notes on the left. This figure is often identified as Wright's friend Burdett, who knew the purchaser of *The Orrery*, Washington Shirley, 5th Earl Ferrers, himself a prominent amateur astronomer and owner of an orrery. Ferrers may have commissioned the painting, via Burdett, and possibly even influenced its design.[70]

Wright's *Orrery* and *Air Pump* (and also his *Gladiator* and *Academy by Lamplight*) underline how a fundamental tenet of the Enlightenment was to promote both the pursuit of knowledge – particularly the relationship between objects and ideas – and, equally important, its broad dissemination through the kind of social gatherings and demonstrations that Wright represented and likely witnessed firsthand. From 1748, for example, James Ferguson (mentioned above) gave public lectures on experimental philosophy, which he repeated in many English towns, including Derby in 1762.[71] The now common idea of the 'public sphere' or 'public realm' was first coined to describe such social developments during the eighteenth century, with the spread of institutions, learned and improving societies, informal groups such as reading and dining clubs, and new spaces for socialising, ranging from coffee houses to annual art exhibitions.[72] The Lunar Society (1765–1813), a dining club of industrialists and intellectuals including Matthew Boulton, Erasmus Darwin, Joseph Priestley and Josiah Wedgwood, has long been associated with Wright (see p. 44). Later commentators have even suggested that Wright's representation of moonlight in his candlelights and 'night pieces' was in part a response to the club's name, which stemmed from its practice of scheduling meetings on the Monday closest to the full moon, thus providing better light for members travelling home.[73]

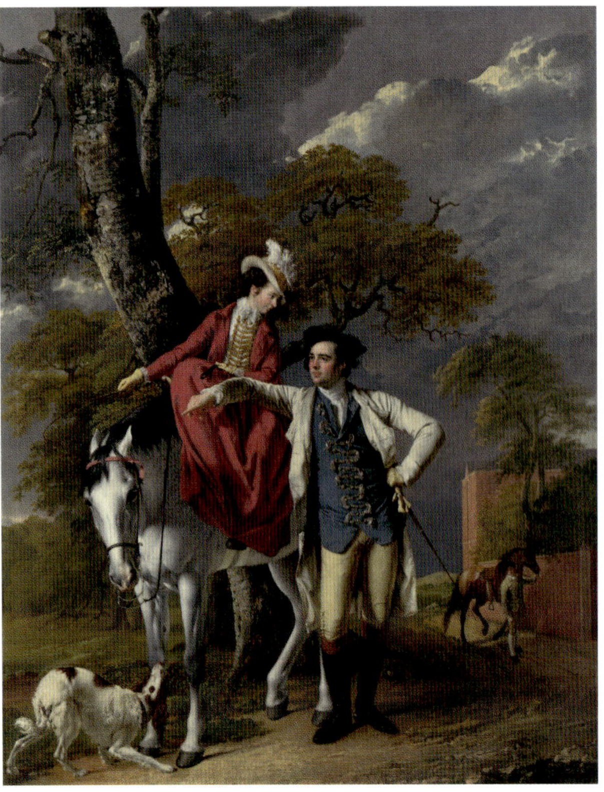

In translating such well-established pursuits and events to a painted canvas, Wright drew not only on the old master traditions previously discussed, but also on the popular style of group portraiture described in exhibition catalogues as 'a conversation'. The small-scale 'conversation piece' typically shows groups of full-length figures who have come together for some kind of convivial or family occasion. Wright painted portraits in this vein, such as that of his friends Mr and Mrs Thomas Coltman (fig. 12),[74] and *An Academy by Lamplight* can be seen as an innovative take on this format. Tellingly, 'conversation' was also applied to large-scale representations with life-size figures, such as Wright's *Burdett* portrait (fig. 3).[75] Within polite society, women (as well as men) were encouraged to engage with natural philosophy, in tandem with art and music, resulting in publications aimed at female readers that followed a conventional format for treatises of a 'dialogue' or conversation, rather than a straightforward narrative: to give but two examples, John Harris's *Astronomical Dialogues between a Gentleman and a Lady* (1719), which contains an illustrated description of 'the famous Instrument, called the ORRERY', and Benjamin Martin's *The Young Gentleman and Lady's Philosophy* (1755), which includes a discussion on using live animals in an air pump.[76] While in Wright's *Orrery*, the young adults, seated across from one another, are shown completely absorbed by the model solar system, in *The Air Pump* the couple to the left of the lecturer have turned to each other, the man's lips slightly parted, perhaps to infer a discreet conversation. The intimacy of this vignette is explained by the fact that the two portrayed are Thomas Coltman (who also owned the paintings shown in plates 9 and 10) and his fiancée Mary Barlow, before their marriage in 1769.

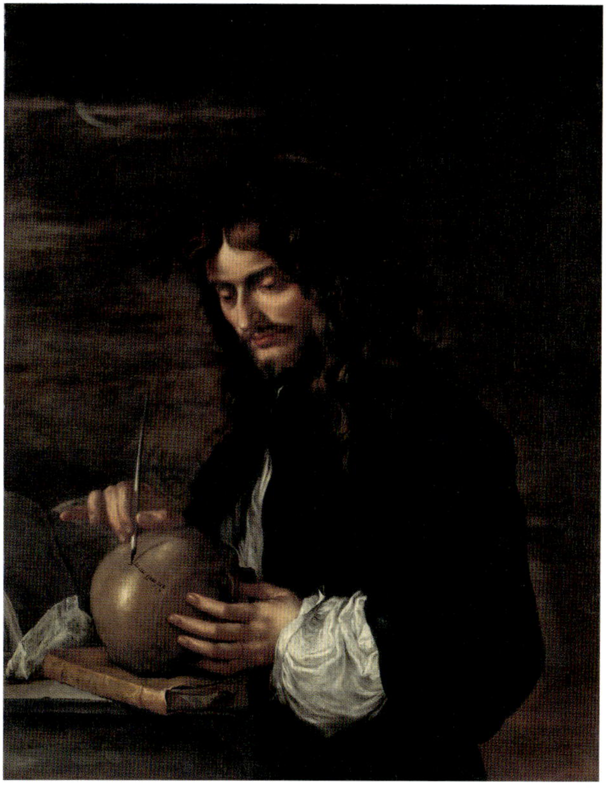

Fig. 12 *Mr and Mrs Thomas Coltman*, about 1770–2, oil on canvas, 127 × 101.6 cm, The National Gallery, London

Fig. 13 Salvator Rosa, *Self Portrait*, about 1647, oil on canvas, 99.1 × 79.4 cm, The Metropolitan Museum of Art, New York

DARKNESS, MELANCHOLY AND THE SUBLIME

In reality, the correlation between light and the pursuit of knowledge was long established in Western art and culture, in both religious and secular contexts. From the early seventeenth century, 'lucubration' (from the Latin 'lucubrare') referred specifically to scholarly or artistic study undertaken at night by candlelight, with associated connotations of virtuous industry and sobriety.[77] Related imagery likewise formed part of the *vanitas* tradition. Characterised by symbolic objects that denote the transience of life – a burning candle, for example, embodies time passing – these paintings were linked to representations of mortality or *memento mori* (Latin for 'remember you must die'), the latter epitomised by Salvator Rosa's brooding self portrait (fig. 13). A talented actor and poet, Rosa shows himself as an intellectual wearing a cypress wreath (an emblem of mourning) and inscribing a human skull (the ultimate symbol of mortality) with the Greek words 'Behold, whither, eventually', which rests on a book by the Roman stoic philosopher Seneca.[78]

Perhaps unsurprisingly, Rosa's landscapes and subject paintings were associated during and after his lifetime with the concept of melancholy, identified in the sufferer (among other symptoms) by profound sadness and/or psychological introspection, sharing similarities to the modern definition of depression. A recurring theme in philosophical discourse, from the Renaissance onwards, was that intellectuals – philosophers, poets and even artists – were not only prone to be melancholic but, through the notion of 'genial' or 'inspired melancholy', were predisposed to genius and exceptional creative ability. The idea that melancholy had a positive side profoundly influenced eighteenth-century medical texts on the subject, one of the most popular being *The English Malady* (1733) by the pioneering Scottish physician and philosopher George Cheyne.[79] As the title indicates, Cheyne argued (as did others) that melancholy was part of the national character, and furthermore that it was specifically associated with wealth, leisure and gentility, and accordingly was a disease of the 'better Sort'.[80] Wright's images of polite self-improvement, for example, include individuals adopting poses associated with melancholy – their head resting on a hand, as in *The Orrery* and *An Academy by Lamplight*, or leaning on a stick or cane, as in *The Air Pump*, where the elder figure (seated on the right) gazes at the shadowy skull, itself positioned directly below the suffering bird.

From the late 1760s, Wright himself was subject to periods of illness and depression, and his self portrait (see fig. 1) – executed at the moment when his fame rested principally on his candlelights – has been described as 'an embodiment of melancholia'.[81] Tellingly, many of the scholars and philosophers exploring the condition over the centuries, from Marsilio Vicino and Robert Burton to George Cheyne, were doing so as fellow sufferers. Wright's approach to his subject paintings may well reflect his own state of mind, alongside wider artistic and cultural trends, such as his incorporation of the moon – a traditional symbol of melancholy – into his work from *The Air Pump* onwards.[82] This is certainly true of the five 'night pieces' representing blacksmith shops (pls 13, 22 and 23) and iron forges (fig. 14 and pl. 24), exhibited (and quickly sold) between 1771 and 1773. These highly innovative and precisely detailed scenes show Wright moving away from interior to exterior (mainly rural) spaces, and away from the single light source of his earliest candlelights. In this he seems to have been adopting and developing a format associated at the time with Vernet, whose Italianate night scenes were particularly admired by British patrons for the atmospheric contrast between man-made light, such as campfires, and the coolness of moonlight. In contrast to Vernet's rustic vignettes, however, Wright makes working-class labour the main focus of his paintings and imbues these figures with individuality, dignity and grandeur, which was highly unusual in European art at the time.[83]

Given the association between melancholy and the leisured classes, noted above, Wright juxtaposes industry and idleness in these scenes with more affluent figures (identified by their dress) adopting meditative poses. Interestingly, work was often promoted as an antidote to melancholy. At the same time, leisure was deemed to be necessary for the proper contemplation of the human condition – ergo by those who could afford the time – with darkness or night as the optimum environment. Relevant here is that, since the 1720s, English poets had been exploring the irrational and uncanny, with early exponents of this new 'gothic' genre nicknamed the Graveyard Poets.[84] Some of the most widely read works, focusing on death, decay and the ruin, were James Hervey's *Meditations among the Tombs and Contemplation of the Night* (1745–7), Edward Young's *Night Thoughts* (1749–51) and Thomas Gray's *Elegy written in a Country Churchyard* (1751). The eerie and often mysterious tone of Wright's scenes of blacksmiths, iron forgers and earthstoppers certainly chimes with this poetic sentiment, in part because some are set in the ruins of a church or abbey.[85]

The concept that aligned itself with gothic and melancholy, and equally constituted a profound break between old and new ways of creating and appreciating art in Britain, was the 'sublime'.[86] While the kind of dramatic effects and devices that came to be expected of sublime images included, for example, sharp contrasts in light and shadow, it was darkness that came into its own

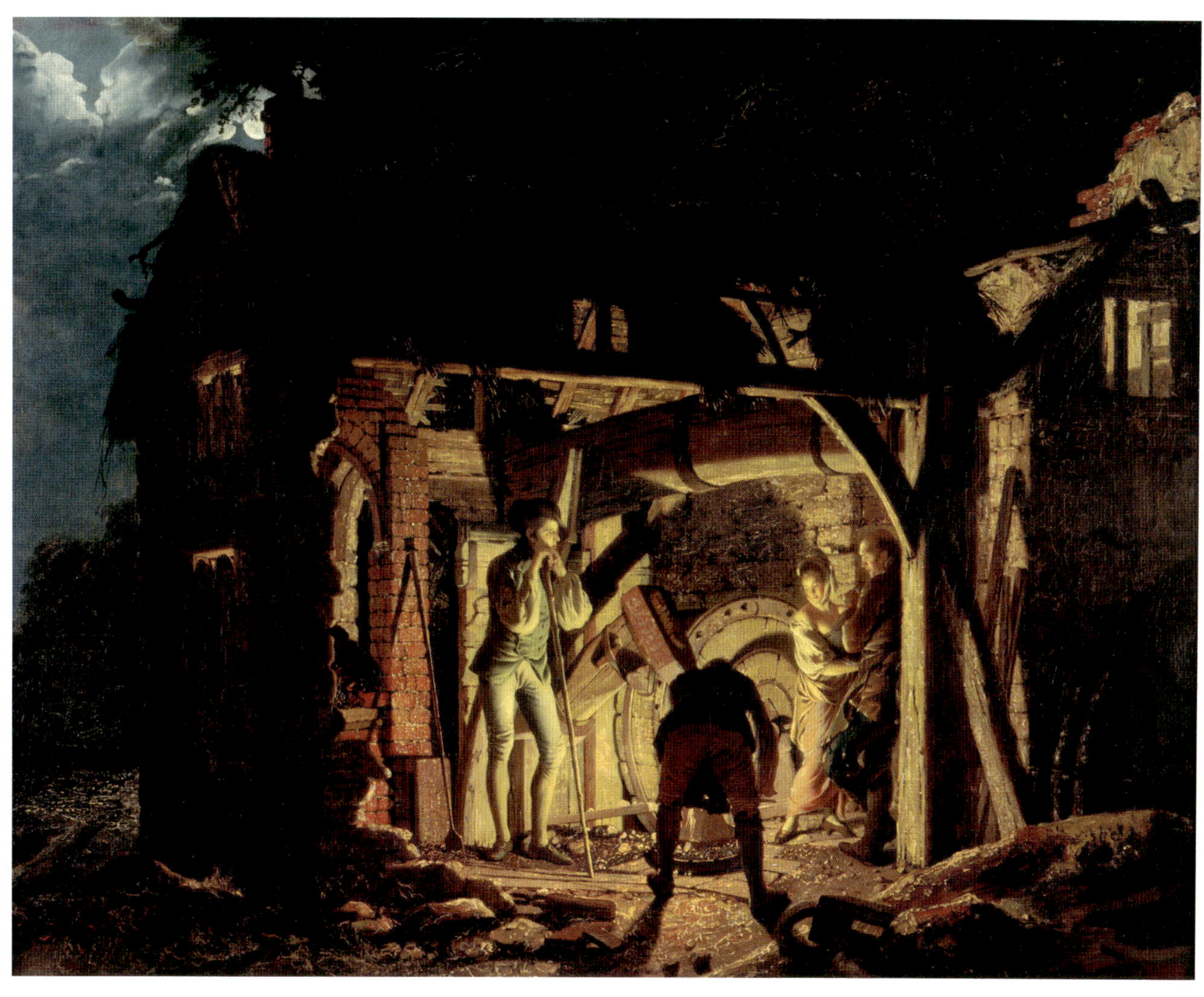

Fig. 14 *An Iron Forge viewed from Without*, 1773, oil on canvas, 105 × 140 cm, The State Hermitage Museum, St Petersburg

as the defining component.[87] Wright's appreciation of the sublime is therefore an important consideration in understanding why he appropriated the seventeenth-century tradition of tenebrism and associated candlelights, and equally how it informed his night scenes from the late 1760s. Moreover, his subject paintings, from *The Gladiator* of 1765 to his *Earthstopper* of 1773, were participating in the ongoing debate and classification surrounding aesthetics – the branch of philosophy that deals with the nature and appreciation of beauty, sublimity and, by the end of the eighteenth century, the picturesque (meaning 'like a picture').[88] Two seminal texts in this regard were published while Wright was based in London: Hogarth's *Analysis of Beauty* (1753) and Edmund Burke's *A Philosophical Enquiry into the Origin of our Ideas of the Sublime and Beautiful* (1757).

The now familiar aesthetic opposition of 'the Beautiful' and 'the Sublime' was a concept that was initially aligned with pastoral and epic poetry, hence references from the seventeenth century onwards to

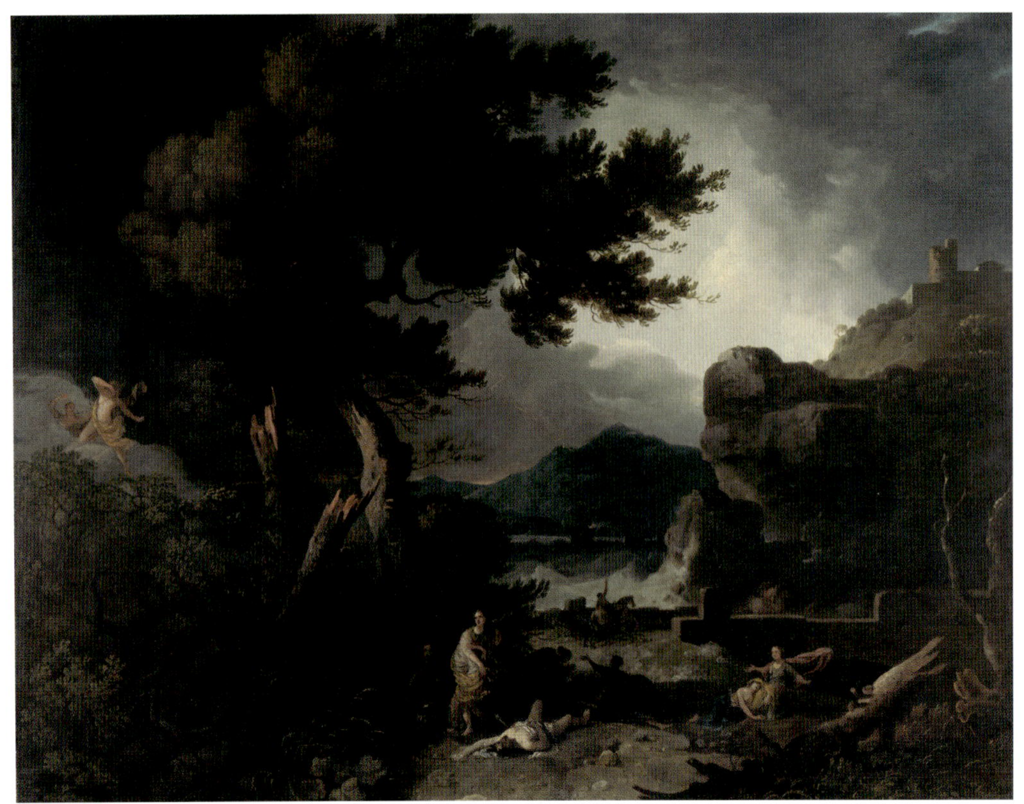

Fig. 15 Richard Wilson, *The Destruction of the Children of Niobe*, 1760, oil on canvas, 147.3 × 188 cm, Yale Center for British Art, Paul Mellon Collection

the 'Sublime of Homer' and the 'Beautiful of Virgil'.[89] By the early 1700s, certain painters were equally seen as exemplars of specific qualities: for example, Claude with beauty and Rosa with the sublime, through their images of luminous calm and savage storm, respectively. While descriptions of the sublime varied, all eighteenth-century commentators agreed that the sensation was premised on the contemplation of powerful scenes or objects, primarily natural phenomena, which aroused feelings of awe and fear in the beholder. Rosa was credited with introducing a new type of expressive landscape to European painting, one that became synonymous with the sublime, because it emphasised dramatic contrasts and vigorous brushwork to evoke wild and rugged scenery, with gloomy skies, blasted trees and rocky outcrops, frequently populated by philosophers, saints and hermits, isolated and deep in contemplation.[90] That British artists were utilising both his figurative and landscape style is evident in Wilson's *The Destruction of the Children of Niobe*, also discussed earlier (fig. 15).

Wright drew direct inspiration from Rosa's *Democritus in Meditation* (see fig. 28) to create the first of his 'outdoor' subject paintings, *A Philosopher by Lamplight* (the title *An Hermit* was used for the mezzotint; pl. 25), possibly encouraged by his lifelong friend and Rosa enthusiast, John Hamilton Mortimer.[91] Echoes of Rosa can equally be seen in *An Earthstopper* (pl. 14), transposed to a local Derbyshire riverbank, with one of the Italian artist's signature motifs, a blasted/dead tree, positioned prominently in the foreground.[92] For comparable reasons, such trees were occasionally incorporated by William Kent, and other architects and landscape gardeners, as sculptural objects in the landscaping surrounding country houses and estates.[93] However, the implication of impending violence and death in Wright's painting is additionally appropriate, given that the job of the earthstopper, acting for the local hunt, was to block up earths (or dens) during the night, forcing foxes to remain in the open to be hunted the following day.

Although Burke was sceptical that the 'imitative arts' (as he described them) could produce an authentic sublime effect, nonetheless he gave some significant hints in that direction by separating the sublime into seven categories: darkness, obscurity, privation, vastness, magnificence, loudness and suddenness, all of which have the potential to shock our sensibilities to the point of disablement.[94] On one level, for Wright to achieve a sublime register in pictorial terms, he simply had to bear these categories in mind. Hence, we can see how *An Iron Forge viewed from Without* (fig. 14) corresponds to 'darkness', 'obscurity' and the natural sublime, just as *The Orrery* evokes the notion of infinity and celestial bodies, and therefore the cosmic sublime.[95] That Wright sought to go beyond mere visual sensation to tackle the concept's psychological dimension (as characterised by Burke) is perhaps most evident in *The Air Pump*: the premise that being confronted by 'pain and danger' and feeling terror (the ruling principle of the sublime), but 'without being actually in such circumstances', results in a kind of intense 'delight' in the spectator.[96] The frisson between fear, pleasure and 'self-preservation' (or survival instinct) is precisely what Stubbs had set out to provoke in his *Horse devoured by a Lion* (see fig. 6). And he continued to exhibit paintings on this theme with great success throughout the 1760s, alongside images of wild and exotic animals.[97] Stubbs's dramatisation of the 'Burkean' sublime may have emboldened Wright to paint – with unflinching accuracy – human beings witnessing an experiment, involving a white cockatoo (a rarity in Britain), deprived of oxygen, near to death. Wright shows the lecturer looking directly at us, his left hand forever poised above the glass container. Will he open the air valve in time? We will never know.

A 'PECULIAR' PAINTER OF CANDLELIGHT

JON KING

On 23 May 1768, after seeing *An Experiment on a Bird in the Air Pump* exhibited at the Society of Artists of Great Britain in London, the *Gazetteer* described Joseph Wright of Derby as 'a very great and uncommon genius in a peculiar way'.[1] The word 'peculiar' later reappeared in William Hayley's *Ode to Mr. Wright of Derby* (1783): 'Thou mighty master of the mimic flame, / Whose peerless pencil, with peculiar aim, / Has form'd of lasting fire the basis of thy fame.'[2] In this period in Britain, 'peculiar' held specific connotations. Before its later associations with 'odd' and 'strange', Wright and his contemporaries would have understood peculiarity as being 'particular' or 'singular'.[3] Indeed, while scenes immersed in candlelight were not wholly original and could be found in Italian, Dutch, Netherlandish and French paintings from preceding centuries, they were not so common among Wright's own generation. By 1772, Wright would be described by fellow artist James Northcote as 'the most famous painter now living for candlelights'.[4] Though produced during a relatively brief period of his career, between 1765 and 1773, Wright's 'candlelights' were recognised as a defining signature 'peculiar' to him, long before his death in 1797.

It is likely that Wright's celebrated candlelight scenes owe much to an early fascination with the principles of illumination and spectacle. Though his childhood is sparsely documented, insights can be derived from notes by his elder brother Richard and the unpublished

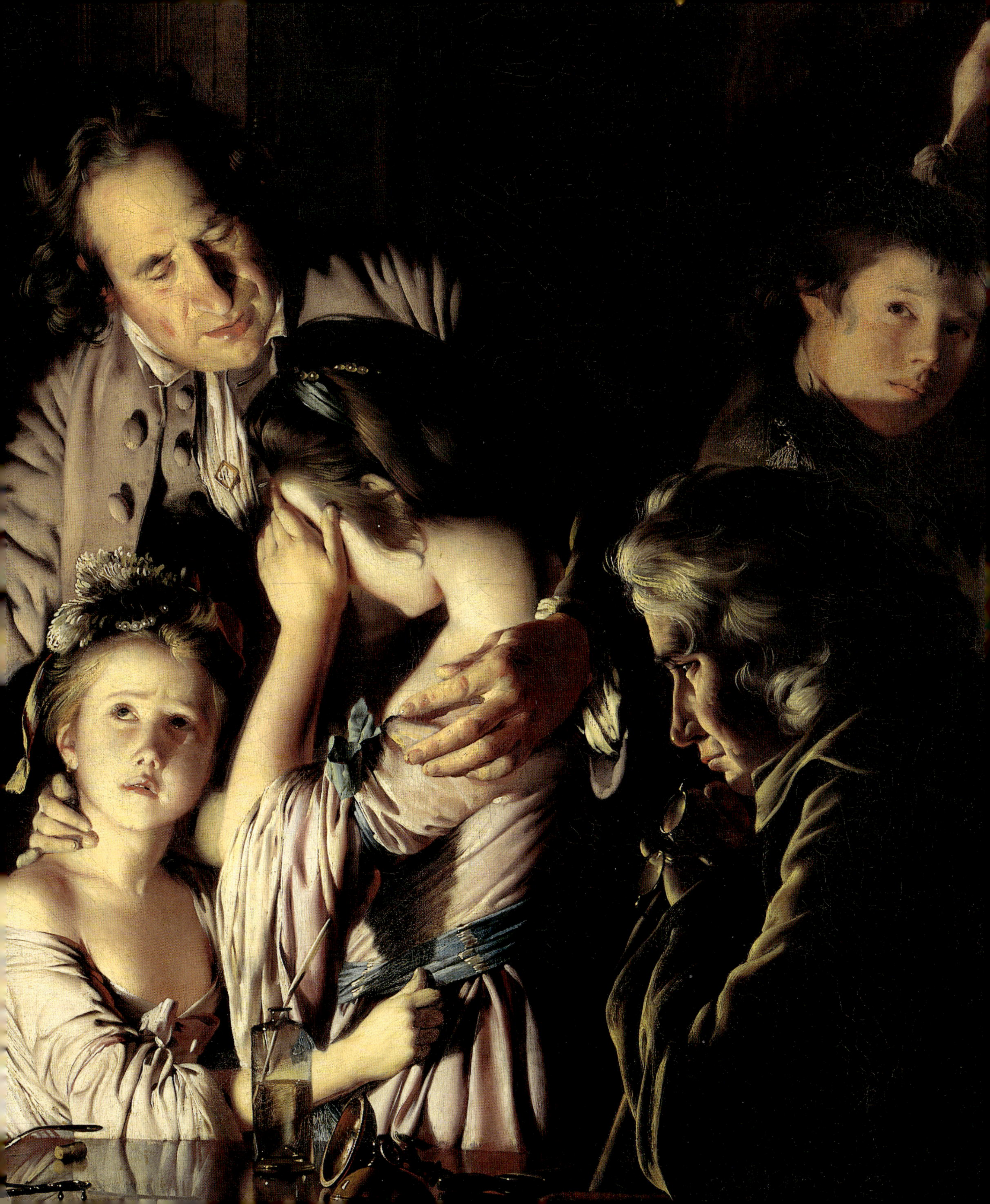

memoirs of his niece, Hannah. According to Hannah, Wright demonstrated a curious and 'active mind' from a young age, spending his free time observing craftsmen at work – such as joiners and marble workers – and recreating what he saw.[5] In addition to noting skilfully made projects such as a chest of drawers, a gun and a clock without a working mechanism, Hannah recounts Wright's early fascination with raree boxes. These portable exhibitions presented unusual images illuminated by candlelight. As a boy, Wright not only grasped the mechanics but, Hannah records, he also impressed and embarrassed the showman with his ingenuity:

> Having seen a raree show, he considered attentively upon what principal it could be formed; having discovered the manner of placing the glasses, he completed a show about three feet high; he then went to the Showman, and told him he had made a show like his; the man would not believe it at first, but upon inquiring how he had made it, he found it was quite right, & begged he would not tell any one by what means he had effected it.[6]

The raree show often employed a magic lantern – an early image projection device originating from the Netherlands that illuminated hand-painted slides onto a wall or screen by passing candlelight through a glass lens. This device could come in the form of a peepshow-like box glowing from within, offering a more intimate viewing experience. This latter form is illustrated by the popular Sèvres porcelain figurine *La Lanterne Magique*, created around 1757, which depicts a girl peering into a lantern while a boy, acting as the showman, operates the device (pl. 16).[7] Widely imitated by British porcelain factories, the figurine highlights the appeal of the magic lantern, demonstrating the playful ingenuity of a child engaged actively with the mechanics of spectacle rather than remaining a passive observer.

Wright's early experiments creating a raree show and the scenes of his mature artistic vision suggest a profound relationship between the experience of childhood wonder and his candlelight scenes. They certainly speak to the kinds of entertainment Wright would have been familiar with as a child: those action-packed miniature worlds of the theatrical peepshow (pl. 15).[8] They are also deeply connected to the broader interest in optical devices that captivated artists both before and during Wright's time. Godfried Schalcken, the seventeenth-century Dutch painter with whom Wright was often compared, created his candlelit compositions using an early form of peepshow apparatus. According to Horace Walpole, Schalcken arranged objects in a darkened room and, 'looking through a small hole, painted by day light what he saw in the dark chamber'.[9] Similarly, Wright himself devised his own viewing contraption in the late 1760s, staging his candlelight scenes to be viewed through a peephole in his well-lit studio.[10]

This technique ran adjacent to other forms of perspectival viewing inherited from seventeenth-century Dutch traditions, such as 'perspective boxes' – comprising interiors of miniature rooms outfitted with painted representations of architecture and furnishings. Artists and viewers in Wright's time were captivated by such experiments with optical devices, which transformed perception and framed the act of looking. The Claude glass – a small, darkened mirror used to soften and recompose landscapes into picturesque views – was another such tool, allowing artists and travellers to see the world through a mediated lens. Engaging with this culture of optical ingenuity, in the 1780s Wright's contemporary Thomas Gainsborough went on to produce a series of landscapes painted in oil on glass, designed to be illuminated from behind by candlelight and viewed through a specially constructed 'showbox'. In addition to Dutch peepshows and magic lanterns, Gainsborough likely drew inspiration from contemporary glass paintings and the 'Eidophusikon', a miniature theatre for the display of pictures invented by the painter Philippe Jacques de Loutherbourg in 1781.[11]

Seen within the context of the growing excitement surrounding optical devices, the composition of Wright's paintings can be compared to the experience of peering into a magic lantern (an optical effect perhaps most explicitly realised in *An Iron Forge viewed from Without*, see fig. 14): both involve immersive participation, capturing the play of light and shadow as communities gather around a candlelit spectacle.[12] Inviting viewers to closely observe an atmospheric, illuminated scene, Wright's paintings evoke the lantern's sense of childhood enchantment, but on a larger and more expansive scale. In this way, they engage fully with acts of looking, allowing viewers to feel as though they are intimate observers. Like a peepshow, they create a 'private drama' that unfolds publicly.[13]

This sense of theatrical observation extended beyond the gallery. Wright's candlelight compositions were widely disseminated through mezzotint prints, connecting them to broader visual culture. Eighteenth-century Britain was defined by an obsession with visuality, spectacle and display, in which seeing and being seen were central to self-definition and social standing.[14] Wright's paintings reflect this visual culture, blurring the boundaries between scientific demonstration, theatrical spectacle and artistic display. Breaking away from the conventions of 'high art', his candlelight paintings embrace popular visual entertainments while transforming them into works of serious artistic ambition. In this way, his works not only responded to but thrived on the evolving culture of mediated observation, turning acts of looking into deeply sensory and immersive experiences – distinctly 'peculiar' within eighteenth-century British painting.

IMPROVING THE CANDLELIGHT GENRE

Perspectival devices were closely tied to a contemporary fascination with light, optics and human perception that offered new, theatrical ways to understand and depict reality. The camera obscura – a small, centuries-old optical instrument that used an aperture or lens to project an inverted image of the outside world onto a surface inside a darkened chamber – brought together the worlds of science and art. It is regarded as a precursor to the magic lantern, and both devices were often compared to telescopes and microscopes for their ability to extend human vision. Informed by Isaac Newton's *Opticks* (1704), they became metaphors for the eye's capacity to capture and interpret the external world. Artistic depictions such as Charles Amédée Philippe van Loo's *The Camera Obscur*a (fig. 16), originally (and incorrectly)

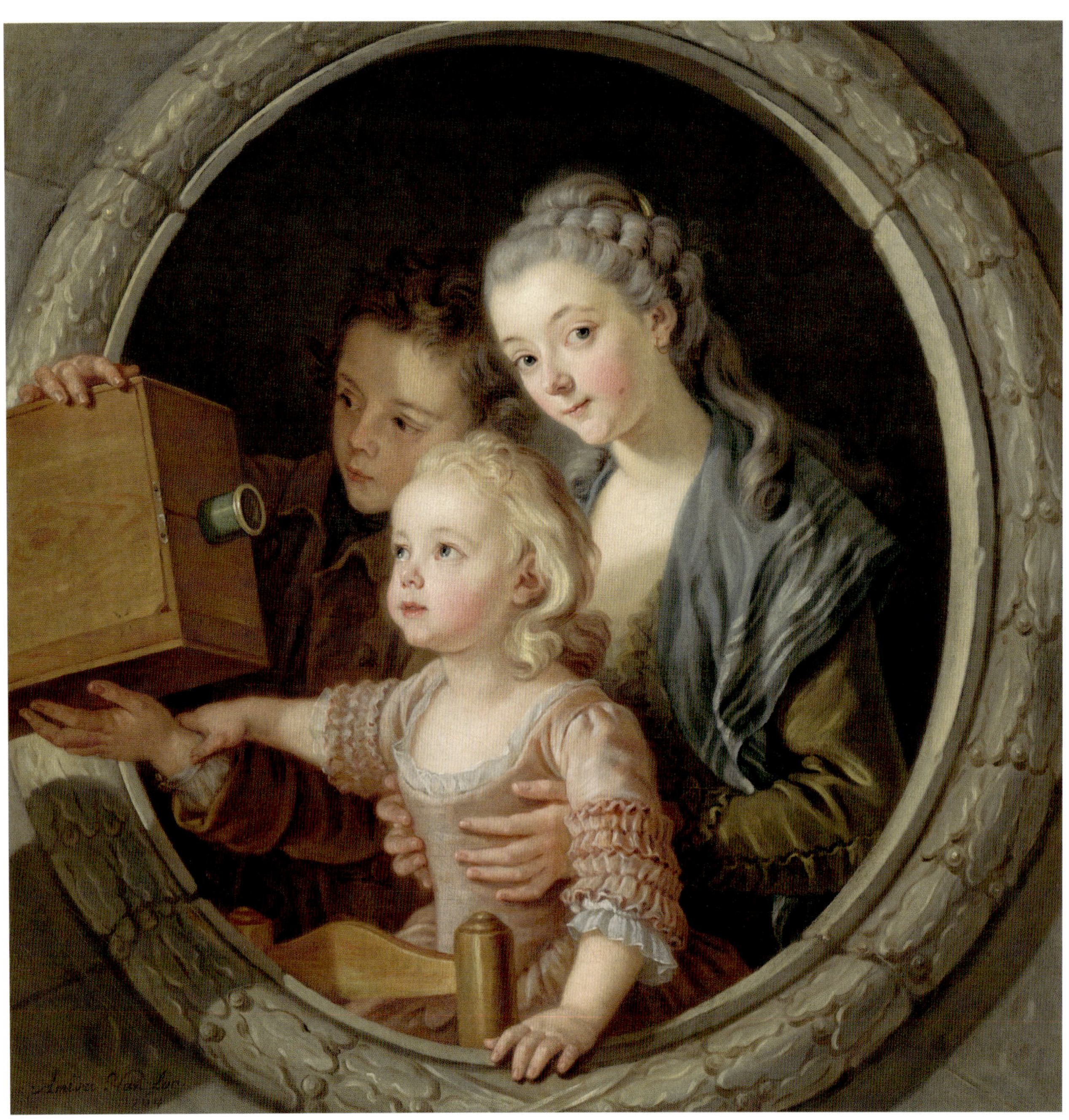

titled 'The Magic Lantern', reflect this fascination. Van Loo's use of a *trompe-l'œil* frame, from which children emerge, cleverly mirrors the interplay of illusion and reality of optical devices like the one held by the young boy. But while the camera obscura and magic lantern were often connected, there was a key difference: the camera obscura was related to the eye's perception, whereas the magic lantern magnified and projected the imagination.[15]

Unsettling the categories between the real and the imagined, Wright may have been aware of contemporary concerns about the magic lantern's impact on children's minds. While the device held educational potential, its association with itinerant performers known as 'savoyards' or 'galantee' showmen, and its use in street performances targeting gullible children and working-class audiences, cemented its reputation as a 'lowbrow' form of entertainment. Unlike Van Loo's painting, which embraced the wonder of the camera obscura, satirical works like Paul Sandby's *The Cries of London – The Magic Lantern Man* (fig. 17) depicted the magic lantern as an amusement for street urchins and the uneducated.[16] Negative depictions of peepshow devices had already been explored by artists such as William Hogarth, who on at least one occasion used the peepshow as a metaphor for distraction and the corrupting influence that acts of 'looking' could have on young minds.[17] At the same time, the concept of 'projection' drew a direct link between such devices and the mind of the artist. In Sandby's graphic etching of Hogarth as a magic lantern from 1753 (fig. 18), we see a parody of the visual satirist, blending man and machine, with a beam of light – emanating from his mouth – cutting across the picture's surface. Magic lanterns, like Hogarth, serve to craft a sensationalised dramatisation of society rather than an accurate reflection of its realities.[18]

As Sandby's prints reveal, candlelit spectacles were a source of wonder and a symbol of a perceived moral impoverishment. This belief carried over into painting, where lamplight was not a subject fashionable for artists in Wright's time, with only a few of his contemporaries showing an interest in this theme. Examples include George Romney, who painted two small, sketchy

Fig. 16 Charles Amédée Philippe van Loo, *The Camera Obscura*, 1764, oil on canvas, 88.6 × 88.5 cm, National Gallery of Art, Washington, DC

Fig. 17 Paul Sandby, *The Cries of London – The Magic Lantern Man*, 1760, etching, 22.2 × 16.1 cm, Philadelphia Museum of Art

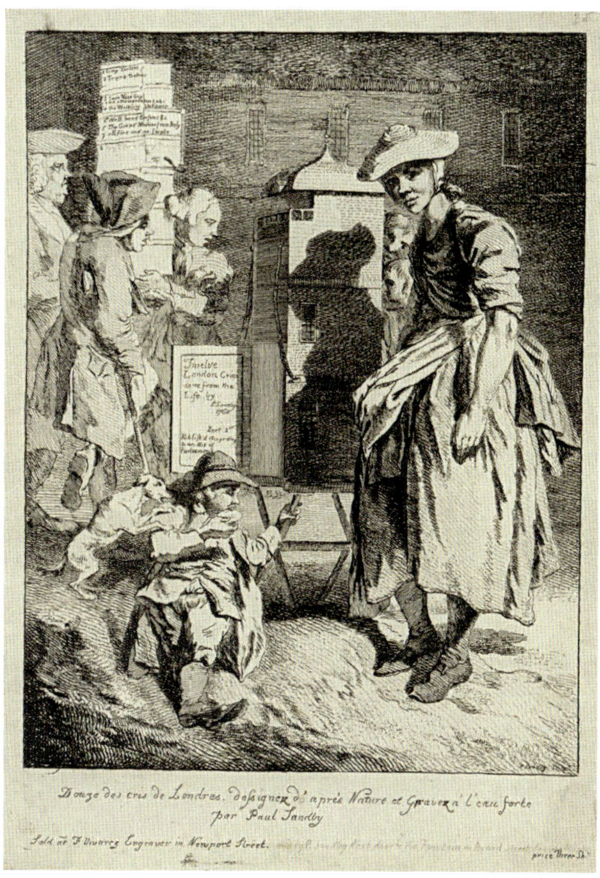

'candlelights' in 1761, and Henry Robert Morland, who repetitively painted coquettish portraits of pretty young girls from the lower classes by candlelight.[19] Morland was undoubtedly influenced by Schalcken, whose pictures primarily dealt in intimate, atmospheric candlelit scenes of a risqué character (fig. 19). Schalcken spent some years working in England, where his paintings remained popular with English collectors, so it is very likely British artists encountered them in person.[20] The influential Walpole openly detested what he perceived as the moral deprivation in such paintings.[21] Walpole's opinion was possibly influenced by a Dutch painter of the previous century, Gerard de Lairesse, who, as an open critic of Schalcken, had equated painterly depictions of lamplight with the taint and vulgarity of 'melancholy, faint, and gloomy' environments.[22]

To establish credibility and recognition, Wright had to accomplish some key objectives as he embarked on his depictions of candlelight scenes in the mid-1760s.

Fig. 18 Paul Sandby, *Satire with Hogarth as a Magic Lantern projecting a Parody of his 'Paul before Felix'*, 1753, etching, 17.5 × 23 cm, Harvard Art Museums/Fogg Museum, Cambridge, MA

Fig. 19 Godfried Schalcken, *Young Man and Woman studying a Statue of Venus, by Lamplight*, about 1688–92, oil on canvas, 43.8 × 34.9 cm, The Leiden Collection

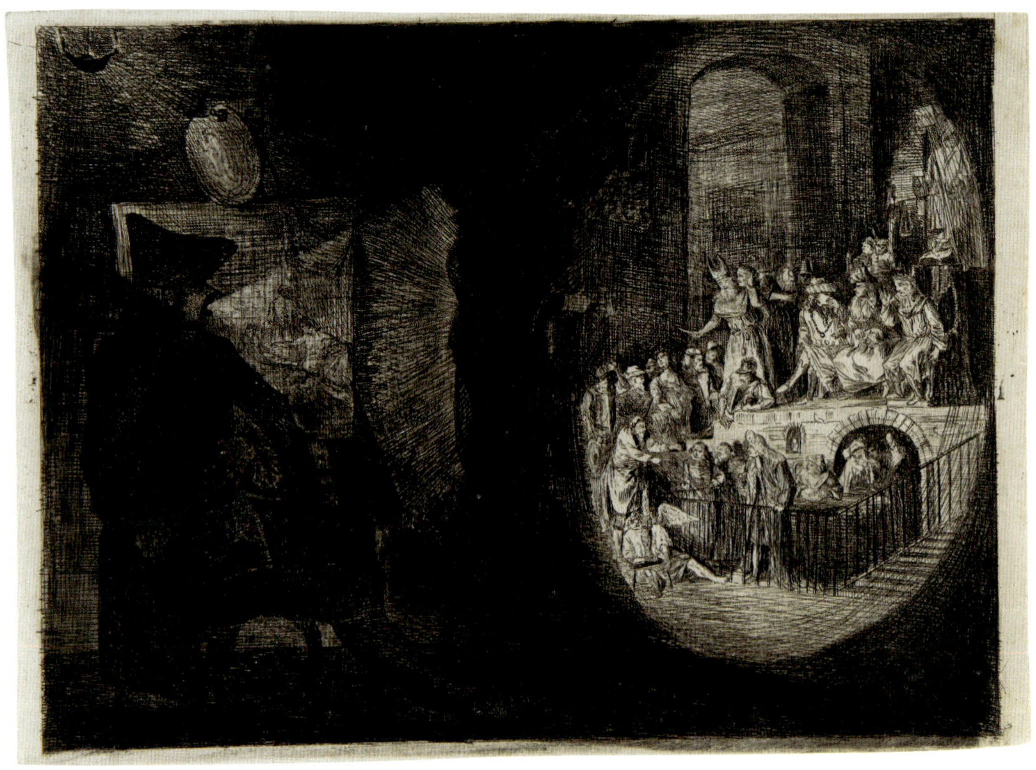

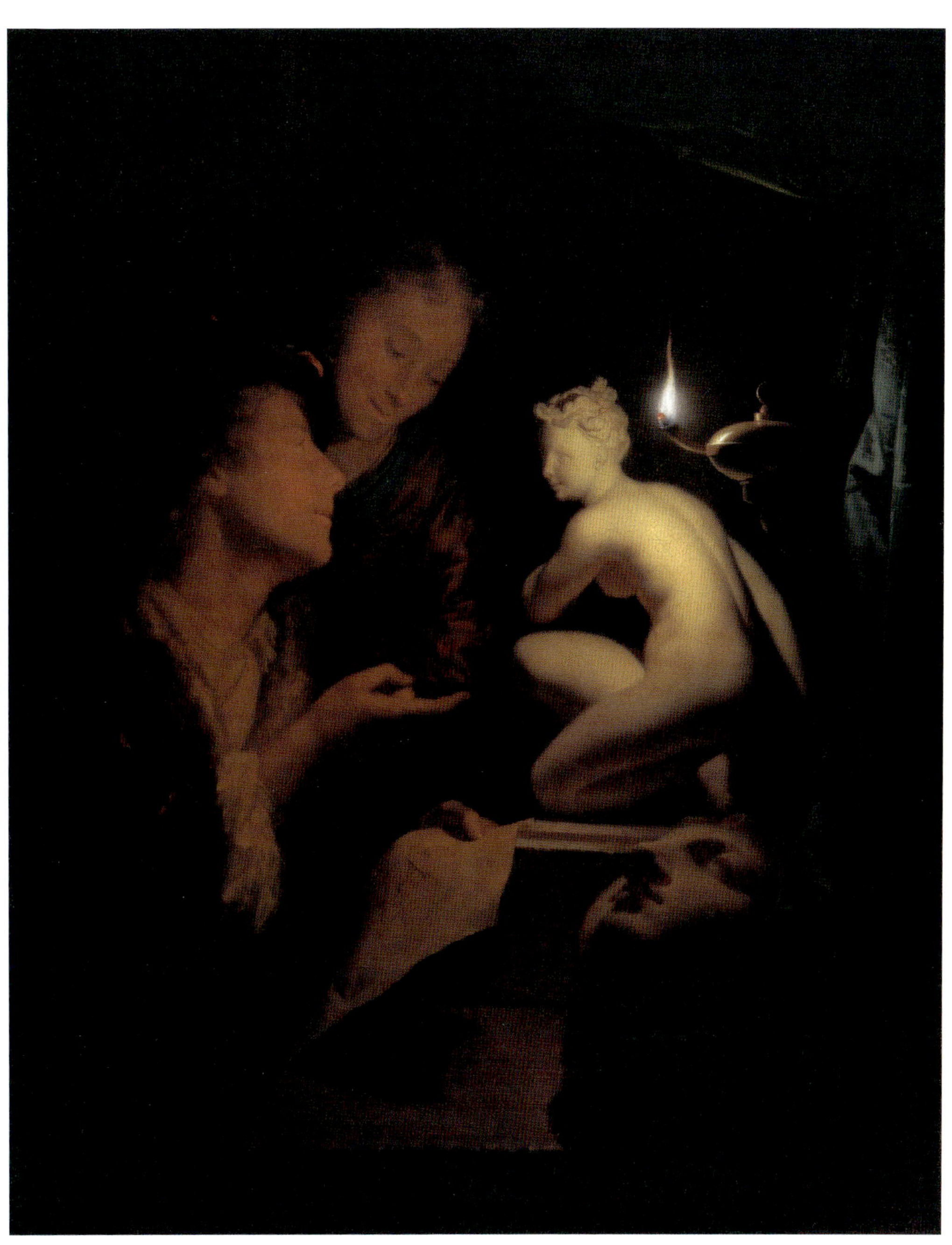

First, he would need to improve the moral sentiment of the genre, removing its traditionally lewd associations by imbuing it with deeper significance. And second, he would need to elevate his works to the philosophical heights of the sublime, using light, shadow and scale to convey complex themes and evoke awe through theatrical, elaborate observation. By doing so, he could transform candlelight scenes from the realm of mere 'genre pieces' or 'conversation pieces' into one equivalent to history painting – the most prestigious genre.[23] His primary method would be to merge the raree showman with the philosopher, and the spectacle with a site of cerebral observation, thereby consolidating popular entertainment with acts of intellectual and moral observation. As with cultural discussions around optical devices like the magic lantern, central to this dynamic interaction would be the figure of the child.

CANDLELIGHT LEARNING AND MORAL REFINEMENT

The first of Wright's candlelight paintings to be publicly exhibited at the Society of Artists, and his national debut, was *Three Persons viewing the Gladiator by Candlelight* in 1765 (pl. 1). Unlike the majority of his later candlelight scenes, which often include children as central figures, this composition focuses exclusively on an assembly of adults. These are all men of Derby. The man on the far right is thought to be a self portrait of Wright, and the person in the middle with his face in full, his friend Peter Perez Burdett, a cartographer and draughtsman who modelled for Wright on many occasions during their friendship between 1763 and 1773 (see also fig. 3). To the left is 'Old John', a resident of the Devonshire alms-houses in Derby, cast as a bespectacled, sage-like teacher.[24] The scene is intimate, with the three men gathered around a plaster cast of the *Borghese Gladiator*, a celebrated icon of classical art and anatomy that was a staple of drawing academies in the eighteenth century (pl. 3).[25] The plaster cast seen in this picture was a modern and fashionable consumer product, with a strong record of educative purposes, as seen in Philippe Joseph Tassaert's *A Drawing Academy*, which he drew the previous year (fig. 20).

Wright's choice of subject reflects a developing discourse on the transformative power of vision. English philosopher John Locke described sight as the most comprehensive of the senses, a gateway to knowledge and morality. Observation, he argued, was an active process – an engagement with the external world that shaped the mind's capacity for judgement and reflection. In Wright's *Gladiator*, this idea is reinforced by one of the men holding up a drawing of the sculpture for assessment, framing the act of looking as a critical, intellectual endeavour. Art historian David Solkin expands on this, suggesting that Wright presents looking as a moral exercise – one that refines the viewer's intellect and character.[26] The intimate arrangement and the use of chiaroscuro – an artistic effect producing strong shadows in bold contrast to areas of light – heighten this sense of contemplation, transforming the study of classical art into a pathway to self-improvement.

Wright would return to depicting classical sculpture later in the decade, but his next significant, and larger, candlelight painting centred on his first scientific apparatus and would earn him considerable recognition. At the time of its exhibition, the full title of the painting was *A Philosopher giving that Lecture on the Orrery in which a Lamp is put in the Place of the Sun* (pl. 5). James Gandon, a contemporary of Wright, noted that during the painting's debut at the Society in 1766, 'for fine effect, it attracted the attention of the visitors at the exhibition more than any other picture that was presented for public

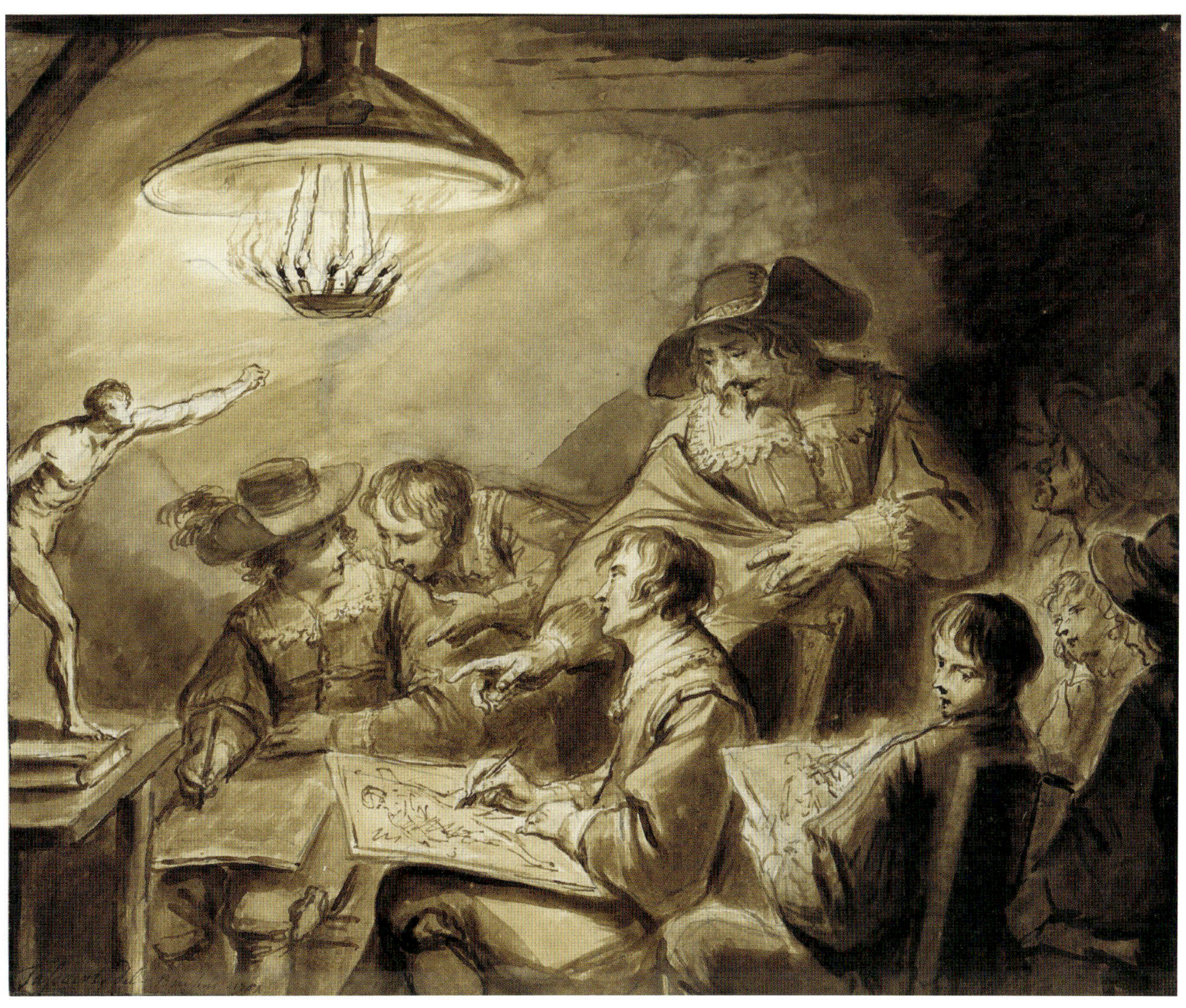

Fig. 20 Philippe Joseph Tassaert, *A Drawing Academy*, 1764, pen and brown ink with brown wash over graphite on paper, 33 × 40.6 cm, The British Museum, London

approbation'.[27] The painting presents a family gathered around an orrery – a mechanical model of the solar system (pl. 7). Its glowing brass orb illuminates the fascinated faces of the children, much like a magic lantern. At the centre of the composition, a natural philosopher presides over the demonstration, elevated both physically and symbolically as an almost divine figure, orchestrating this spectacle of the heavens.

Despite the painting's overt engagement with scientific instruments, Wright's connection to the world of science was less direct than is often assumed. Though his friend Burdett, who also appears as a model in *The Orrery*, had ties to the Lunar Society, Wright himself was never an active participant in the Birmingham-based group's discussions or experiments. His fascination lay not in the scientific method itself but in its theatricality, its potential to transform knowledge into spectacle. As scholar Matthew Craske has pointed out, by naming 'that lecture' in the title, Wright's painting refers to a particular event in which the orrery's central orb was replaced with a lamp to simulate an eclipse – an effect designed to be experienced in a darkened room, heightening the drama of revelation in the manner of a camera obscura.[28] In this way, Wright's work aligned less with scientific enquiry and more with the visual culture of optical entertainment. For many eighteenth-century viewers, such images carried religious overtones, reinforcing the idea that studying the heavens was akin to contemplating the divine. As the astronomer James Ferguson wrote in 1760, the orrery's purpose was 'to explain the Laws by which the Deity Regulates and Governs all the Motions of the Planets'.[29] Wright's painting, then, did not merely depict an instrument of reason; it staged a moment of sublime awe, where observation became a spiritual act.[30]

Two years after *The Orrery*, Wright produced a larger and even more emotionally charged composition, *An Experiment on a Bird in the Air Pump* (pl. 6). Again, a scientific demonstration takes centre stage, but here the focus shifts from celestial order to human response. A single candle, hidden behind a glass vessel, casts deep shadows across the scene, heightening its drama. At its centre, the philosopher – eerily illuminated – assumes a near-supernatural presence, presiding over the bird's fate with calculated detachment. Like his counterpart in *The Orrery*, he appears more god-like than scholarly, orchestrating an unsettling act of revelation while directly propositioning the viewer. Wright once again places children at the heart of the composition, amplifying its emotional stakes: while one girl clings to her sister in distress, a young boy watches with fascination, absorbed in the mechanics of the demonstration rather than the fate of the struggling bird. Here, as before, Wright's interest lay not in the science itself, but in its power to provoke, to stir curiosity, wonder and unease. The philosopher has the air of a travelling showman who will soon pack up his box of tricks and move on to another household. By translating such moments into immersive, candlelit dramas, Wright transformed the apparatus of learning into the language of spectacle – crafting images that, much like the magic lantern, blurred the boundaries between knowledge and entertainment.

If we look at Wright's preparatory sketch for *The Air Pump*, the relationship between the experiment and the girls' reactions is far more pronounced (fig. 21). Very few of Wright's painted sketches have been documented, making this one particularly valuable in understanding the evolution of this significant work.[31] The philosopher and his air pump are sidelined to the edge of the scene, while the two girls are centralised. Even though the final composition introduces more spectators and thus a greater variety of reactions, from this sketch it is evident that the distress of the two girls was an important

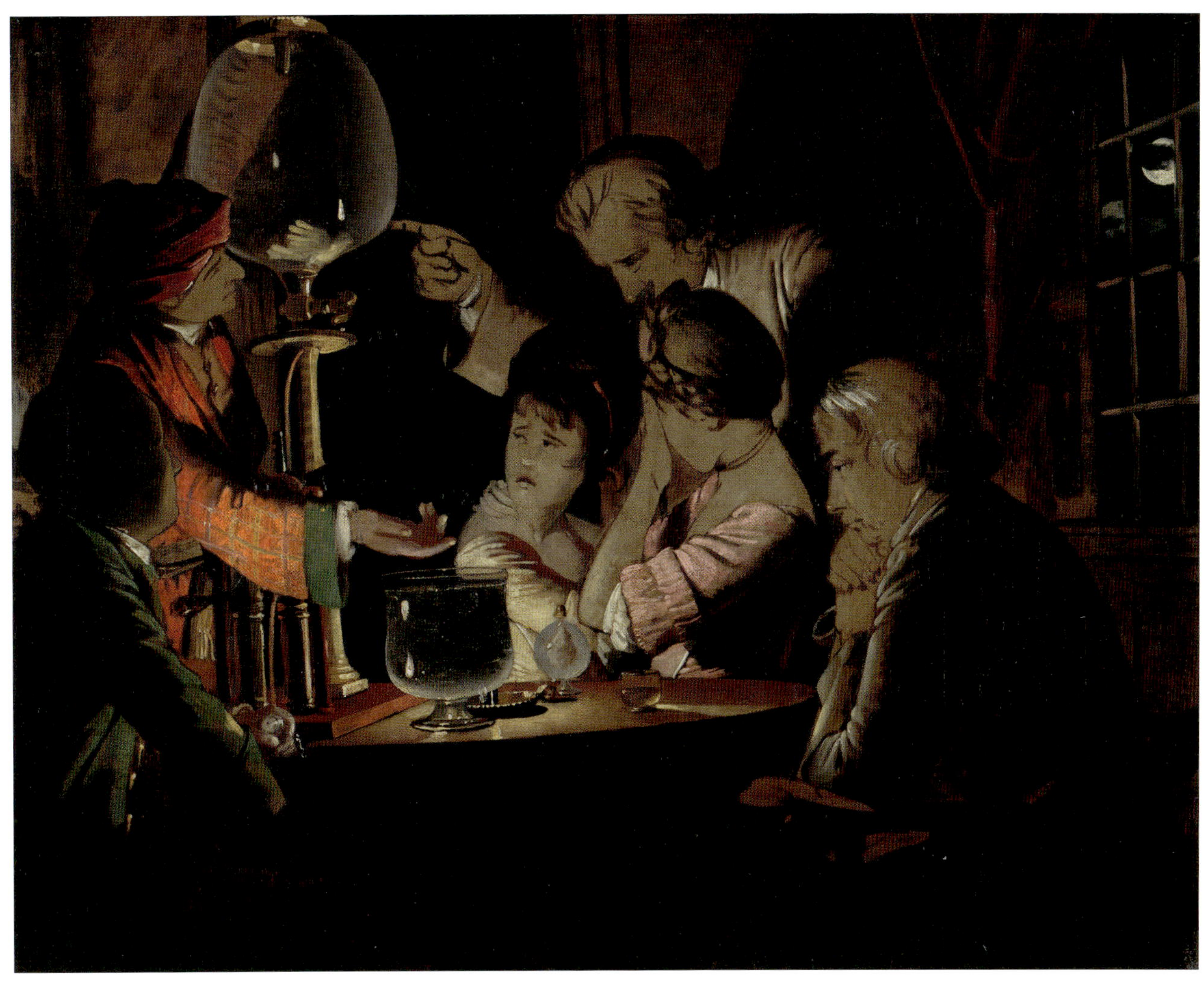

Fig. 21 Study for *An Experiment on a Bird in the Air Pump*, about 1767, oil on canvas, 63.5 × 76.2 cm, Derby Museums

linchpin for Wright's original idea for the painting.[32] Unlike *The Gladiator* and in some ways *The Orrery*, which focus primarily on a group of educated, like-minded men of art and science, the reaction of the young girls introduces a new theme within Wright's candlelight genre: the moral and ethical implications of looking.

Fig. 22 William Pether after Godfried Schalcken, *Studious Society*, about 1760–80, mezzotint, 30.4 × 25 cm, private collection

Fig. 23 Arthur Devis, *The John Bacon Family*, between 1742 and 1743, oil on canvas, 76.2 × 131.1 cm, Yale Center for British Art, Paul Mellon Collection

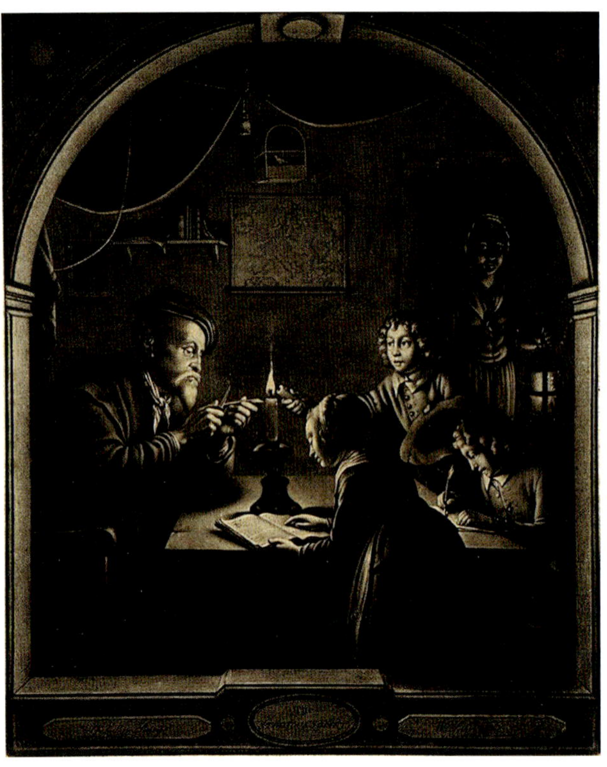

DOMESTIC EDUCATION

Both *The Orrery* and *The Air Pump* show scenes that take place within the home, offering a clear reflection of the eighteenth-century preference for domestic education over institutional schooling. As Solkin contends, the presence of children in Wright's candlelight paintings reinforces the nurturing values of eighteenth-century family life being expressed by philosophical thinkers of the time. Adam Smith, for instance, advocated that to improve both 'domestic morals' and 'domestic happiness', parents needed to raise children who were 'dutiful to their parents'. To achieve this, Smith warned parents not to send their boys off to 'distant great schools' and 'young ladies' off to 'distant nunneries and boarding-schools', but instead to 'educate them in your own house'.[33]

Visual representations of domestic learning of this kind precede Wright. Indeed, if Schalcken is to be considered his forerunner, then we might more readily look to his *Studious Society* – engraved into mezzotint by William Pether, who also engraved Wright's candlelights (fig. 22). Here, as in Wright's compositions, domestic education is tied to the father figure. This is symbolised by the young boy lighting his candle from his father's, while the mother's lurking presence is revealed only by the gentle glow of her lantern in the dark doorway (in Wright's candlelit scenes of learning, mothers are completely absent).[34] Echoing the subject of *The Air Pump*, a birdcage on the wall (this time above a geographical map) offers a vehicle to express the family's 'exotic' interests – a symbol of imperial wealth and global exploration. The home becomes a microcosm of domestic bliss and of empire, where grandiose ideas are condensed into a cosy family space and a practical learning environment.

Inspired by Dutch art of the seventeenth century such as this, eighteenth-century British art saw a shift towards

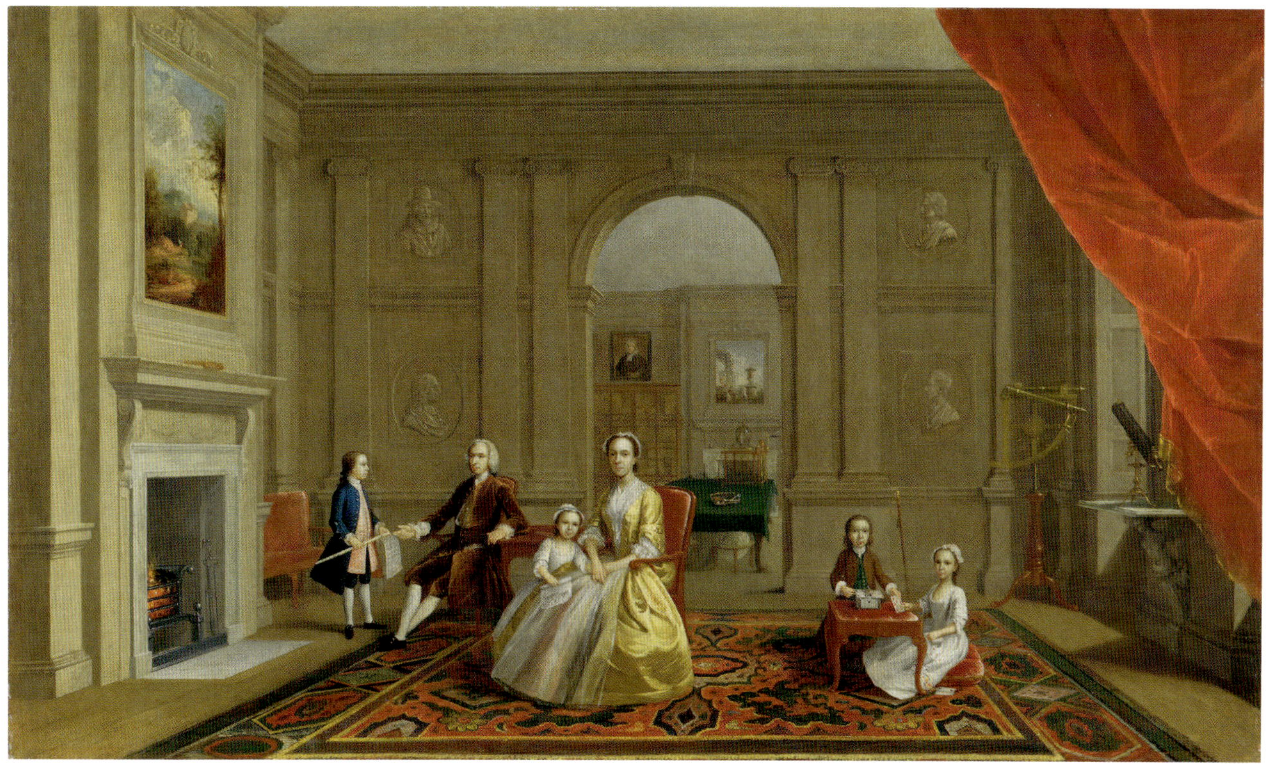

depictions of children's roles within the domestic sphere, particularly engaging with activities of learning and intellectual curiosity alongside adults. These depictions often took the form of 'conversation pieces' – a genre featuring groups of people in informal settings, designed to foster social interaction and encourage viewers to engage in conversation about the depicted scene. One artist who helped popularise this genre was Arthur Devis, as seen in *The John Bacon Family*, where children participate in intellectual discovery under paternal guidance (fig. 23). The father, rooted in the Northumbrian gentry, is positioned as an authoritative figure of learning, reinforced by the telescope and transit quadrant by the window, and the table-mounted air pump seen through the archway. In the words of Peter de Bolla, the painting emphatically declares 'Man of Science!', linking paternal intellect to familial order and education.[35]

But where do Wright's candlelights sit within such depictions of children in domestic education? Like those by Schalcken and Devis, Wright's scenes of scientific learning – *The Orrery* and *The Air Pump* – evidently take place in wealthy residents' private houses. But while he and other artists of the period depict intellectual enquiry within the family home, Wright's approach is distinct. His candlelight scenes are not primarily about the arrangement of grouped figures but about the act of looking itself.[36]

And the child observer symbolises the fragility of innocence and the precarity of moral development. We might therefore view Wright's candlelight scenes, and especially *The Air Pump*, as anticipating a variation of the magic lantern that would emerge towards the end of the eighteenth century: the phantasmagoria.

Fig. 24 Jean Ouvrier after Johann Eleazar Schenau, *La Lanterne Magique*, 1755–84, engraving, 48.4 × 34.9 cm, Yale University Art Gallery, New Haven, CT

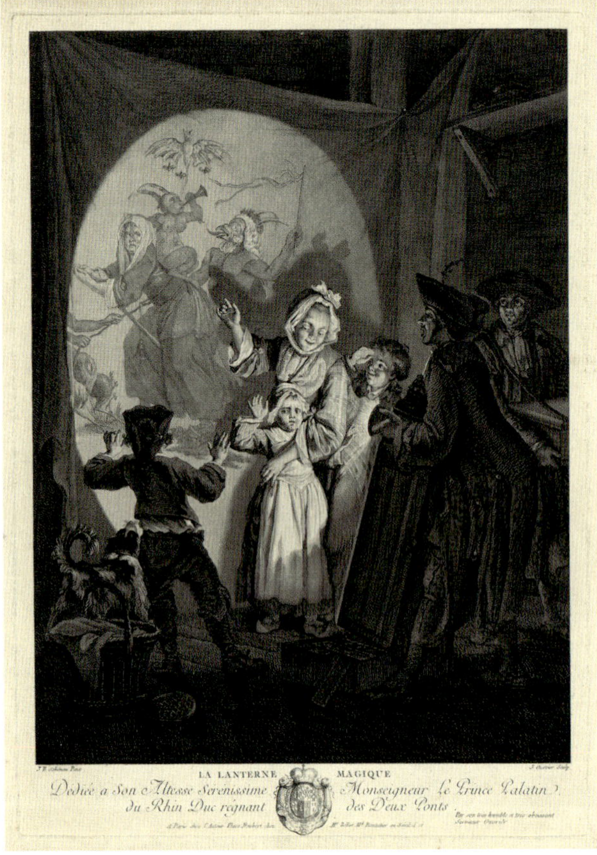

Held in darkened rooms to amplify fear, the phantasmagoria was a public show in which a magic lantern projected terrifying imagery onto a screen or a wall. The lantern's association with 'visual magic' meant the phantasmagoria came to symbolise a widespread sense of losing stability and reality in contemporary life. An effective illustration of this type of spectacle can be found in an engraving by Jean Ouvrier after Johann Eleazar Schenau, titled *La Lanterne Magique* (fig. 24).[37] Here, the distress of the young girl is comparable with that of the girls in *The Air Pump* – except this time, rather than her father urging her to look, it is her mother, and instead of the private realm of the home, this is a public spectacle. In this respect, the phantasmagoria is a world apart from Wright's serious, high-minded tableaux of art objects and scientific experiments observed within upper-class domestic settings. Yet in both, the complex emotions attached to human curiosity and wonder are expressed primarily through the reaction of children, emphasising the moral implications of looking. Moreover, a lingering tension surrounds the figure of the 'philosopher', whose role as the orchestrator of spectacle encapsulates both the sensationalism and the moral ambiguity of a showman. Wright's candlelight paintings thus employ the emotive resonances of light spectacles like the magic lantern to offer a deliberate departure from traditional depictions of domestic learning.

SENSORY EXPERIENCE

Wright's nighttime scenes of children gathered around candlelit objects and animals link to eighteenth-century ideas about childhood and the senses, particularly those of philosopher Jean-Jacques Rousseau. Rousseau believed that early sensory experiences shape a person's understanding of the world. His ideas built on Locke's concept of the newborn's mind as a *tabula rasa* (blank slate), and that people learn primarily through what they see. In his book *Emile, or Treatise on Education* (1762), Rousseau argued that a child should be surrounded only by useful objects, writing that 'everything that surrounds him is the book in which, unconsciously ... he continually enriches his memory'.[38] In Wright's candlelight compositions, his choice of objects and the varied reactions of children symbolise how memory and sensation, as Rousseau proposed, play a foundational role for moral and intellectual development. In doing so, they reflected the public's mixed feelings of wonder and apprehension towards new knowledge.

Wright expanded on these themes in *An Academy by Lamplight* (fig. 25), where he replaces the learned adults seen in *The Gladiator* with a group of young students gathered around a classical Roman sculpture. Some boys are sketching, while others lean in closely, their expressions ranging from deep concentration to quiet contemplation. The warm, diffused lamplight casts soft shadows over the smooth surface of the object in front of them – a cast of the Borghese *Nymph with a Shell* (pl. 4). This sculpture evokes the myth of Pygmalion, the Roman tale of a sculptor who falls in love with his own ivory statue, which then comes to life.[39] Often linked to Venus, the nymph symbolises the power of art to inspire transformation and desire – an idea reflected in the longing gaze of the boy on the far left.

Exhibited at the Society of Artists in 1769, *An Academy* offers a subtle commentary on the upheaval taking place in the London art world at the time. A year prior, tensions within the Society caused a group of prominent artists such as Joshua Reynolds and Thomas Gainsborough, led by architect William Chambers and others, to defect. Seeking royal support for a new institution, they approached King George III, who agreed to their proposal and tasked Chambers with drafting a charter outlining how this new academy would be structured. This resulted in the founding of the Royal Academy of Arts, which quickly became the most prestigious institution for artistic training and exhibition in Britain. But its formation marked a shift towards a formalised, hierarchical system, replacing the more inclusive and collaborative spirit of earlier organisations like Hogarth's St Martin's Lane Academy. While it provided stability and royal endorsement, it also introduced exclusivity, limiting opportunities for artists outside its inner circle.[40] Wright, who exhibited regularly with the Society of Artists, was not among the founding members of the Royal Academy. Though his initial reaction is unknown, later letters suggest he was unsettled by the changes. In the autumn of the same year, he left London for Liverpool, possibly in response to the upheaval.[41]

An Academy by Lamplight can be seen as a quiet critique of this new institutional structure. Instead of portraying a rigid, authoritative art school, Wright envisions a more organic and self-directed space for learning. The absence of an adult instructor reinforces the idea that artistic knowledge can be cultivated naturally through observation and experience, rather than imposed from above. This vision stands in contrast to the Royal Academy's structured approach, making Wright's painting an exploration of art education on the one hand, while, on the other, it is a reflection on broader changes happening in the British art world at the time.[42]

The painting presents the transformative act of artistic observation. At its centre, the Borghese nymph serves not just as an object of study but as a catalyst for intellectual and moral growth. In some ways this calls to mind philosopher Étienne Bonnot de Condillac's idea that knowledge develops through sensory experience, as outlined in his *Treatise on the Sensations* (1754).

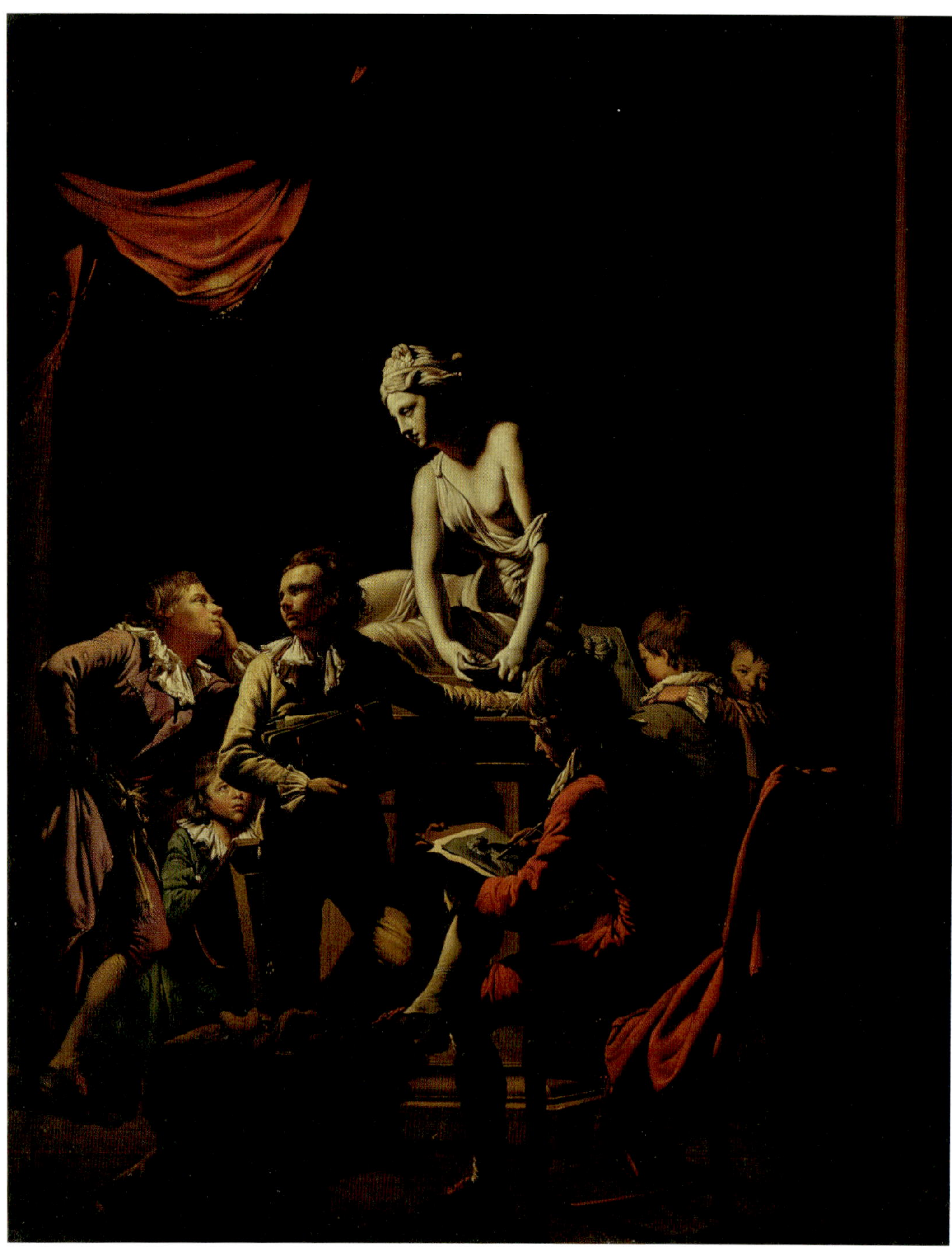

Condillac, also following Lockean ideas of a *tabula rasa*, imagined a marble statue gradually awakening to knowledge through the activation of its senses.[43] Yet, where Condillac bypasses childhood's emotional and cognitive biases by imagining a rational adult statue, Wright turns the dynamic on its head: here, it is the children who experience revelation through sensory engagement with the sculpture. In line with Rousseau, Wright is suggesting that the boys' youthful ardour – often associated with unruly passions (as depicted by Schalcken) – can be transformed into self-discipline and decorum through the refining influence of art.[44]

Wright develops this further in the second version of *An Academy by Lamplight* (pl. 2), painted slightly later though also exhibited at the Society the same year. Here, he revives the *Borghese Gladiator* in the background of the composition, evoking the intellectual, masculine authority of his first exhibited candlelight. Unlike *The Gladiator*, however, no teacher is present in either version of *An Academy*. The boys must interpret and engage with art independently, reinforcing the idea that true learning comes not from rigid instruction, but from active exploration and sensorial discovery.

INNOCENCE AND MATURITY

In the eighteenth century in Britain, new cultural and philosophical attention towards children in art and society made childhood central to understanding the human subject. Artists such as Hogarth, Reynolds and Gainsborough helped to shape an idealised vision of childhood, often portraying children as 'innocent' and distinct from adults, devoid of explicit social class markers and aligned with a sanitised middle-class ideal of moral purity.[45] Other depictions of childhood evolved to reflect both innocence and the complexities of life. These often drew upon seventeenth-century Dutch artistic traditions, in which artists frequently used animals and children's play as a metaphor for broader human experiences, artfully juxtaposing societal conventions with youthful vitality. Works such as Judith Leyster's *A Boy and a Girl with a Cat and an Eel* (fig. 26), for example, use children to playfully explore themes of

Fig. 25 *An Academy by Lamplight*, 1769, oil on canvas, 127 × 101.6 cm, private collection

Fig. 26 Judith Leyster, *A Boy and a Girl with a Cat and an Eel*, about 1635, oil on wood, 59.4 × 48.8 cm, The National Gallery, London

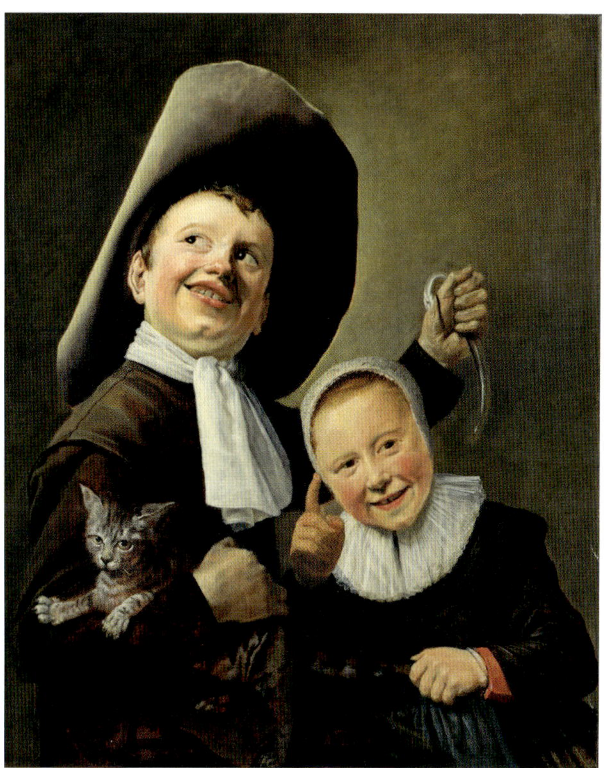

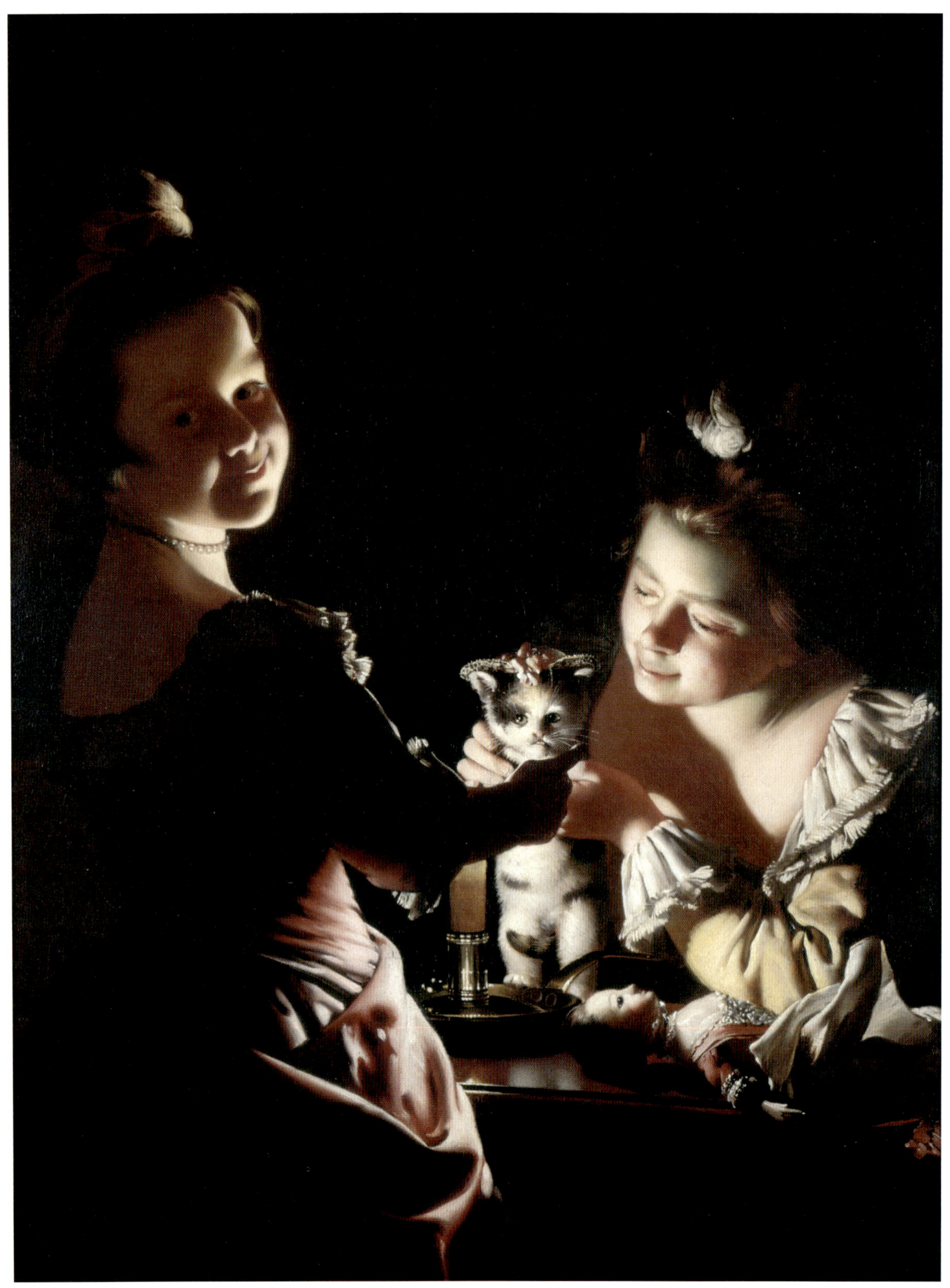

mischief and morality.[46] These present children as vivacious and deeply human, engaging in both lively antics and peaceful domestic moments. Replacing the traditional putto with the 'little perisher' marked a cultural shift toward representing children as distinct individuals, not merely mini-adults or sinful beings in need of reform.[47]

It is within this artistic tradition that we can firmly place Wright's series of candlelight 'fancies', in which he depicted children and animals in imaginative domestic scenes. Fancies cropped up in Wright's candlelight oeuvre relatively frequently in the period between 1767 and 1773, perhaps due to their growing popularity in the art market. Some of these focused on lascivious, intergenerational compositions, such as *A Girl reading a Letter with an Old Man reading over her Shoulder* (pl. 9). Others focused on a curious series of boys playing with pigs' bladders – used as balloon-like toys at the time – lit from behind by a concealed candle. In *Two Boys fighting over a Bladder*, the children wrestle, one silhouetted while the other's squirming facial expression is illuminated by the same source of candlelight (pl. 10). This is a momentary glimpse of mischief: the candle on the table has been knocked over, implying that it might be imminently extinguished and the room plunged into darkness. The scene is ambiguous: in one sense, it portrays a playful, everyday moment of domestic life; in another, it is a moral lesson about greed.

The moralising themes of the fancy picture continue into another of Wright's compositions from this period, *Two Girls dressing a Kitten by Candlelight* (fig. 27). Here, the kitten is dressed in a discarded doll's clothing, while in the process the girls encourage it to stand on its hind legs like a human. Both children smile, one looking at the kitten and the other towards the viewer – as if we have entered the room to interrupt this prankish act. Far from appreciating their efforts, the kitten appears helpless in its distress. We might compare this to *The Air Pump*, which also shows an animal tortured in the centre of the scene. This time, however, a subtle tension is introduced: the girls find pleasure in watching the animal in a state of helplessness, presenting a more menacing aspect of childhood and the fragility of innocence in their hands.[48] As a result, art historians have rightly placed this painting within the tradition of allegories of the cruelty of children, as seen in the first plate of Hogarth's series of four engravings, *The Four Stages of Cruelty* (1751), in which a group of boys conduct a tableau of cruel acts on cats, dogs and birds.[49] However, the painting also belongs to a broader visual tradition of seventeenth- and eighteenth-century imagery that uses cats as symbols of sexual innuendo, particularly in depictions of girls. Beneath its surface innocence, the scene thus carries a mischievous playfulness with subtle erotic undertones, aligning it closely with the works of Schalcken.[50]

Fig. 27 *Two Girls dressing a Kitten by Candlelight*, about 1768–70, oil on canvas, 89 × 69 cm, Kenwood House, London

Around the same time as his fancy pictures, Wright produced other candlelight scenes that continued to explore themes of age, discovery and exposure through seeing. Centring around intergenerational relationships, these works contrasted young and old figures to juxtapose innocence with maturity and wisdom. In *A Philosopher by Lamplight* (pl. 11), exhibited as *The Hermit* at the Society of Artists in 1769, Wright depicts an elderly philosopher contemplating a human skeleton under the glow of a lamp. It shows a *memento mori* – an image designed to reflect on mortality and the transience of life. The composition draws on Salvator Rosa's well-known *Democritus in Meditation* (fig. 28), but Wright introduces a pair of youthful observers peering from the darkness.[51] Their curiosity contrasts with the philosopher's apparent ennui, emphasising youthful wonder and enquiry.

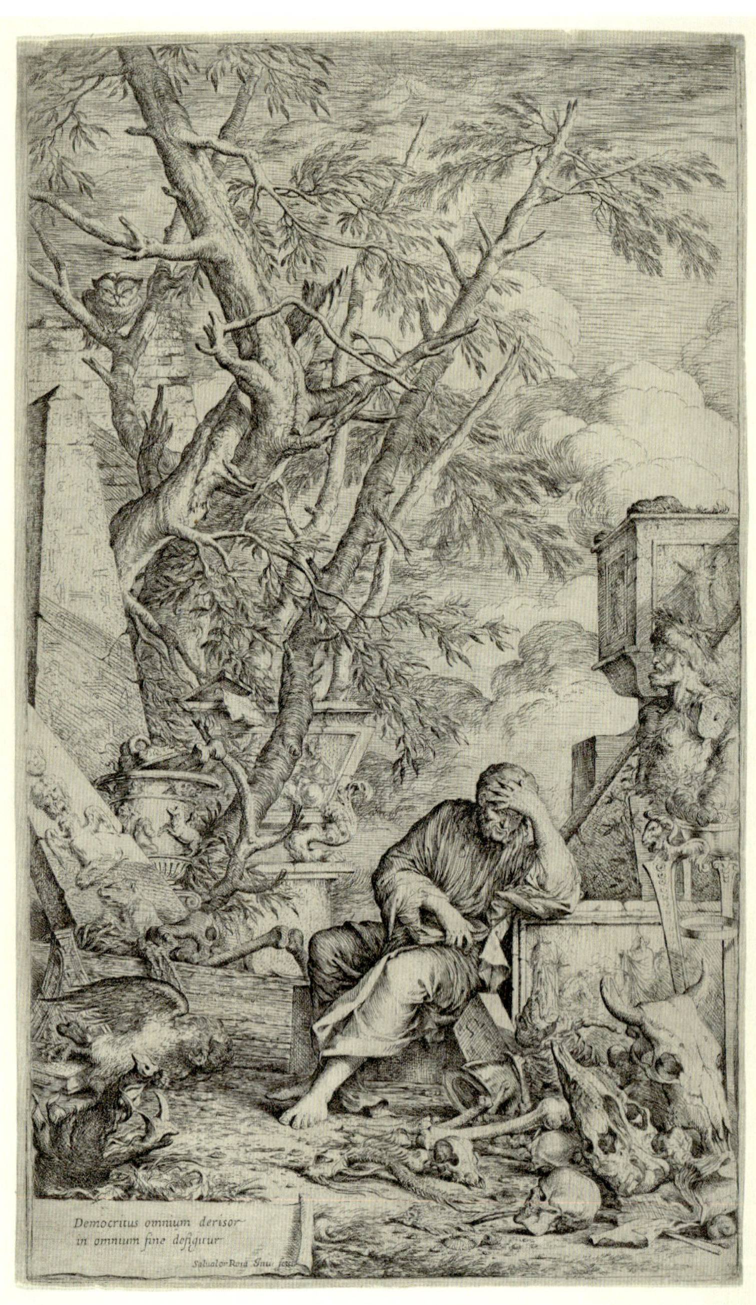
Democritus omnium derisor
in omnium fine defigitur
Salvator Rosa Inu. fecit

Two years later, Wright painted *The Alchymist* (pl. 12), in which the mood shifts from ennui to revelation. Presenting a quasi-religious devotion to nature's sublime truths, Wright portrays the aged philosopher in a pose of reverence, kneeling before the glowing reaction of phosphorus. Far from revealing a new scientific advancement, the scene imagines a historical event, when alchemist Hennig Brand discovered phosphorus in 1669 – over a century before Wright's painting. The philosopher's awe at the chemical reaction is mirrored in the transfixed gaze of a young boy, whose face is illuminated by the candle directly in front of him. Like *The Hermit*, the painting depicts not just an elderly scholar engrossed in his nocturnal investigation, but also a younger boy who takes an observational position. A middle-aged man is introduced who, standing between them, offers a marker to the passage of knowledge across generations. Acting as a bridge between youthful curiosity and elder wisdom, he glances back at the candlelit boy from the shadows, perhaps recognising the wonder he has left behind.

CREATING A LEGACY: THE ART OF DISSEMINATION

Wright faced difficulties in selling *The Hermit*, but he sought to overcome these by commissioning a mezzotint reproduction, engraved by William Pether as *An Hermit* in 1770 (pl. 25). To maximise its appeal in the print market, he had *The Alchymist* engraved by Pether as a companion piece, titled *An Alchymist*, in 1775 (pl. 26) – a strategic move perhaps designed to boost sales through the popularity of a pairing.[52] For Wright, mezzotint prints not only provided lasting records of his major works, but could also be extraordinary works of art in their own right, exhibited alongside his paintings at the Society of Artists.[53] They serve as a crucial link to Wright's engagement with broader eighteenth-century visual culture, where prints, magic lanterns and raree shows operated within a shared visual economy that blurred distinctions between 'high' and 'low' art. Like raree shows, prints played a dynamic role in visual spectacle, often displayed in shop windows and backlit like lanterns to create immersive, participatory experiences for their audiences.[54] As we learned from Sandby's depiction of Hogarth, the performative nature of magic lantern shows, guided by a showman, parallels the way mezzotints were contextualised and mediated through their creators or sellers, drawing viewers into collective acts of spectatorship on a broader scale.

Fig. 28 Salvator Rosa, *Democritus in Meditation*, 1662, etching with drypoint, 46.8 × 28.2 cm, The Metropolitan Museum of Art, New York

During the late eighteenth century, England's print trade expanded rapidly, with London surpassing Paris to establish itself as the leading hub for printmaking.[55] Prints were essential for building an artist's reputation, as they were more affordable than original paintings, widely circulated and central to artistic discussions. Wright understood the importance of public exposure and saw the exhibition of prints, as well as his original paintings, as his marketplace.[56] To reach a wider audience, he commissioned top engravers to produce high-quality mezzotints of his paintings, which became a strategic tool to promote his work and establish his reputation.

Made by rocking a spiked tool across a metal plate to create an entire surface of pits that hold ink, then smoothing areas to varying degrees, mezzotints were a popular medium in the eighteenth century for producing a range of rich, velvety tones. Paintings employing chiaroscuro were therefore ideal subjects for the mezzotint engraver. The technique was seen by Wright's contemporaries as particularly suited to candlelit scenes, allowing the engraver to carve out areas of light from shadow, echoing the natural play of illumination in such settings.[57] When Wright debuted the first of his candlelight series, *The Gladiator*, in 1765, he therefore began to provide engravers with compositions exceptionally well suited to the mezzotint process – a medium they eagerly embraced.[58]

Wright's first painting to be engraved and exhibited at the Society of Artists was in fact not *The Gladiator* but *The Orrery*, reproduced by Pether in 1768 and published by John Boydell in the same year (pl. 19). This masterpiece and its mezzotint helped secure Wright's acclaim and was soon followed in 1769 by Valentine Green's engraving of *The Air Pump* and Pether's engraving of *The Gladiator*. Recognising the financial potential of Wright's candlelit nocturnes, Boydell became a key promoter of his mezzotints between 1768 and 1774, commissioning or acquiring works such as *The Orrery* (pl. 19), *The Air Pump* (pl. 20), *A Blacksmith's Shop* (pl. 23), *An Iron Forge* (pl. 24) and *Miravan* (pl. 27). *Two Girls dressing a Kitten* was engraved by Thomas Watson and published by Watson & Dickinson on 20 February 1781 (pl. 21).[59] These prints, often hailed as exemplary works of English craftsmanship, maintained their appeal in the international market well into the nineteenth century.[60] While Wright's financial gains remain unclear, mezzotints were integral to his fame and, in fact, it is widely accepted that he crafted his candlelight paintings with mezzotint reproduction in mind.[61]

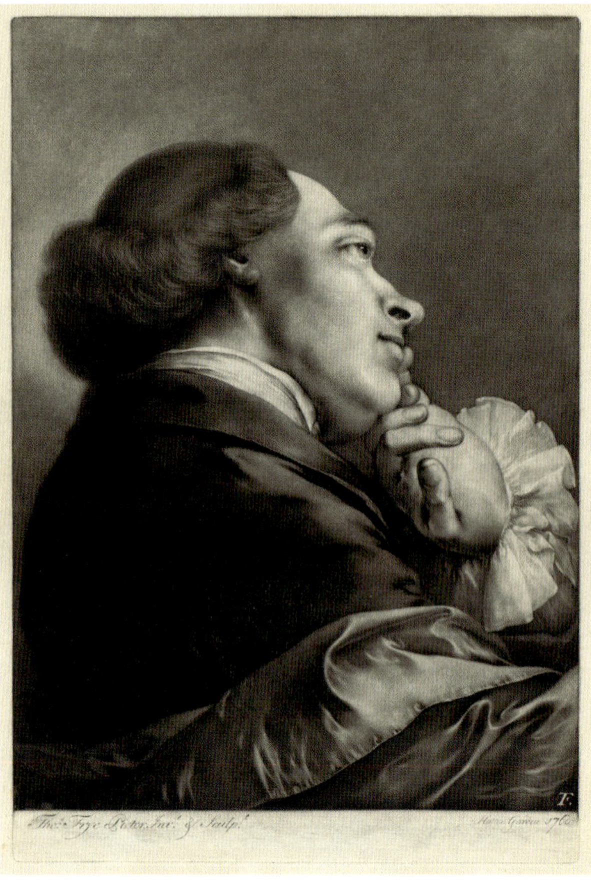

The connection between Wright's candlelight scenes and mezzotints goes beyond technical compatibility to his thematic and compositional choices. Scholars note Wright's debt to engraver Thomas Frye, who taught and later partnered with Pether.[62] Frye's 'character heads' – a series of life-size, candlelit mezzotints (1760–2) – transformed portraits of everyday people into studies of emotion and contemplation, influencing Wright's work in the following decade. This is evident not only in figures like 'Old John of the Devonshire alms-houses' in *The Gladiator* and the boy in *The Air Pump*, whose expression mirrors Frye's *Man wearing Cloak* (fig. 29), but also in the entire cast of *The Air Pump*, where each figure carries the expressive spirit of Frye's studies. Frye himself was influenced by Giovanni Cattini's etchings after Giovanni Battista Piazzetta, which often contrasted portraits of youth and age (fig. 30). Under Pether, mezzotints evolved to convey emotional depth through such contrasts, appealing to a refined, literary audience.[63]

Wright's mastery of candlelight found its perfect complement in the mezzotint. Through this medium, he secured his reputation and expanded his audience, allowing his nocturnal dramas to circulate far beyond the exhibition, extending into both the shop window and the domestic space. As with the raree show, his engagement with this medium had deep roots: as a child, he retreated to the attic of his family home to practise drawing in secret, where he likely copied prints of other artists' work to train his eye in the fundamentals of composition. By layering pencil and washes of diluted ink, he taught himself how to build depth and form through tonal contrast – an instinct that would later find full expression in his candlelight paintings and their mezzotint reproductions.[64] This connection is evident in his many portrait studies, including *Self Portrait in a Black Feathered Hat* (fig. 1), where he meticulously employed pastel to explore dramatic lighting and texture, mirroring the tonal subtleties of mezzotint.

This early curiosity about the power of light to shape perception translated into compositions that did more than depict; they immersed. Whether in the flickering glow of a scientific demonstration, the wide-eyed wonder of a child at the edge of discovery, or the intimate hush of intergenerational learning, Wright's candlelight scenes elevated the act of looking into a profound and deeply human experience. Bridging the gap between art and popular spectacle, between philosophy and entertainment, he crafted a pictorial world that was at once intellectually rigorous and emotionally resonant. By harnessing the tools of dissemination – both the physical medium of the mezzotint and the visual language of theatrical display – Wright ensured that his 'peculiar' vision of candlelit revelation would continue to enchant, provoke and inspire for years to come.

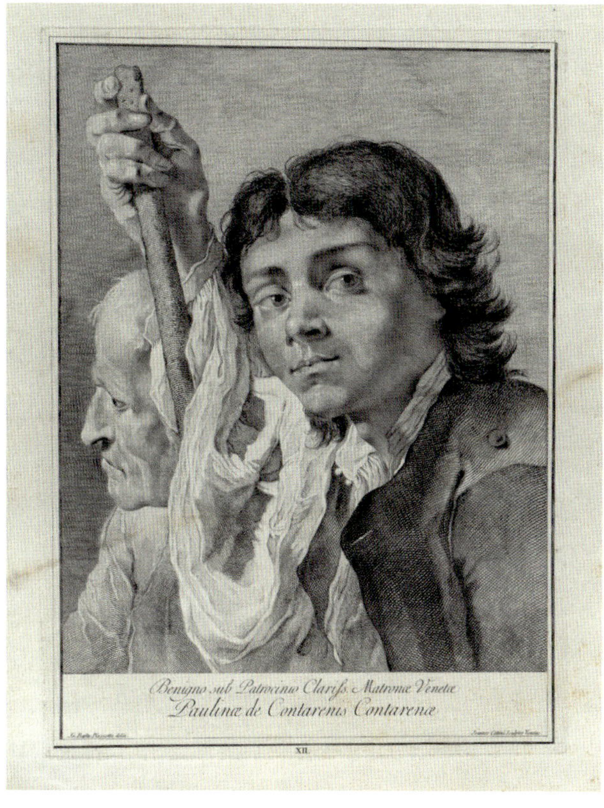

Fig. 29 Thomas Frye, *Man wearing Cloak*, 1760, mezzotint, 50 × 35 cm, Rijksmuseum, Amsterdam

Fig. 30 Giovanni Cattini after Giovanni Battista Piazzetta, *A Young Man leaning on a Staff looking Outward*, 1743, etching, 50.5 × 39.4 cm, The Metropolitan Museum of Art, New York

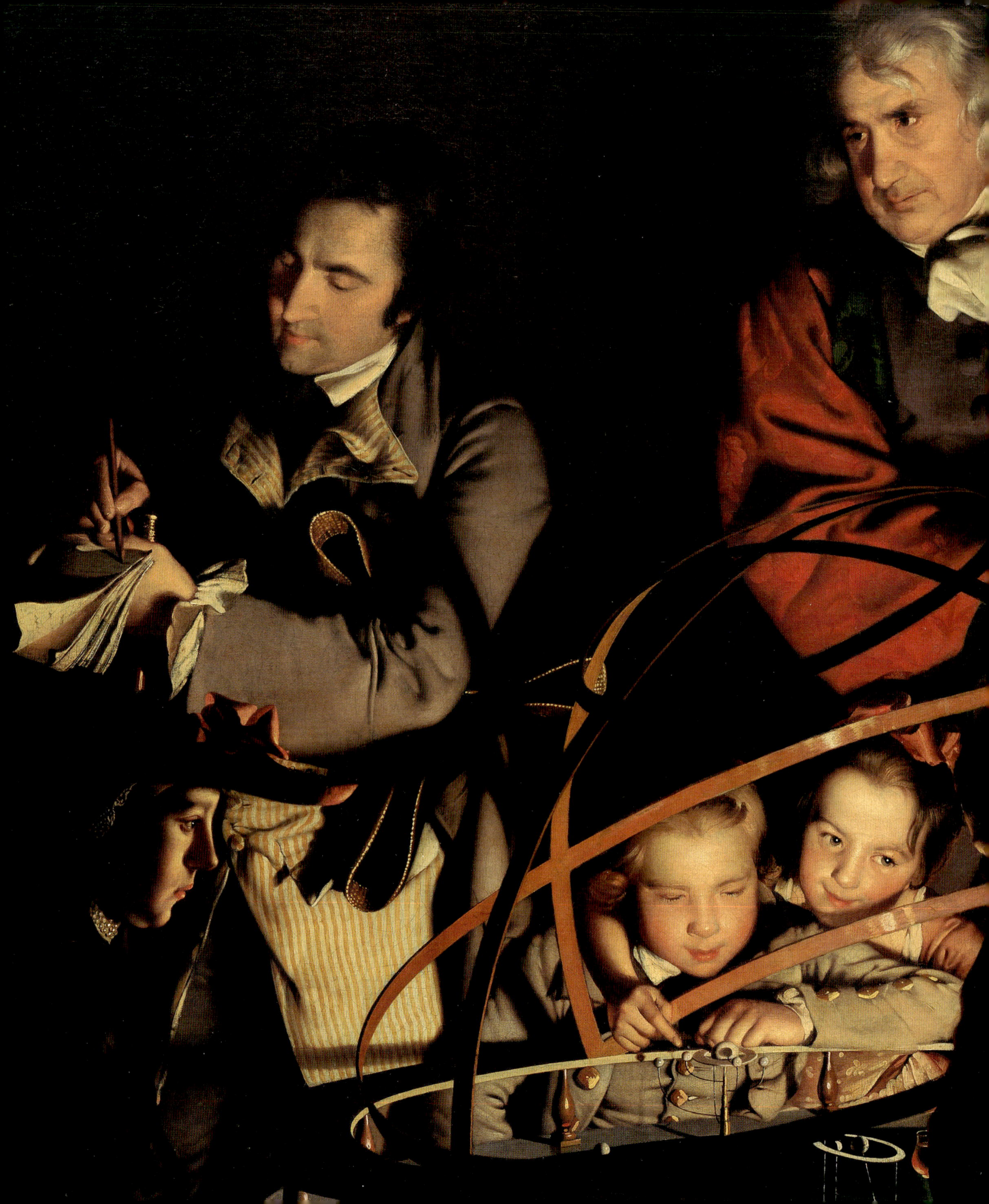

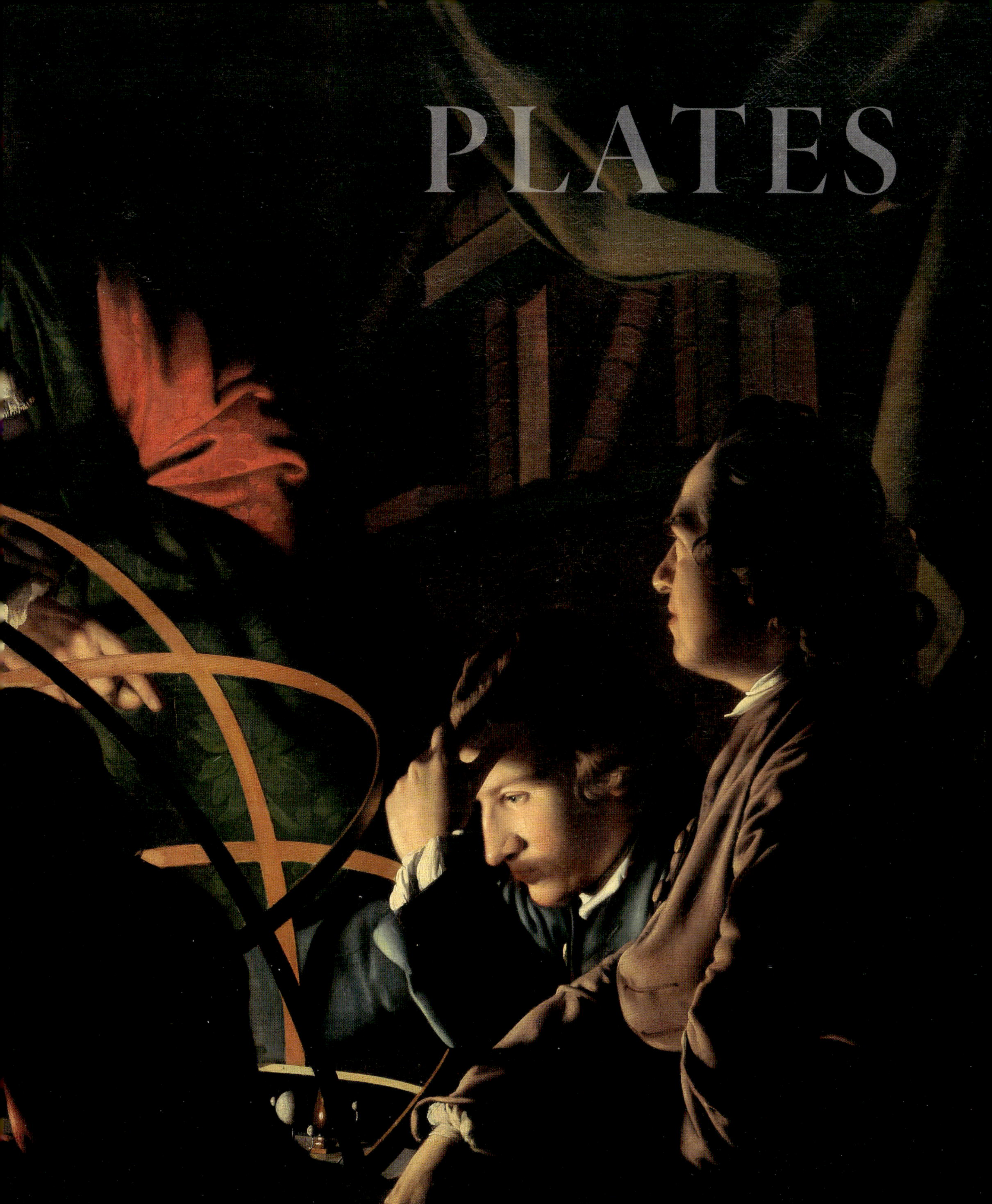

PLATES

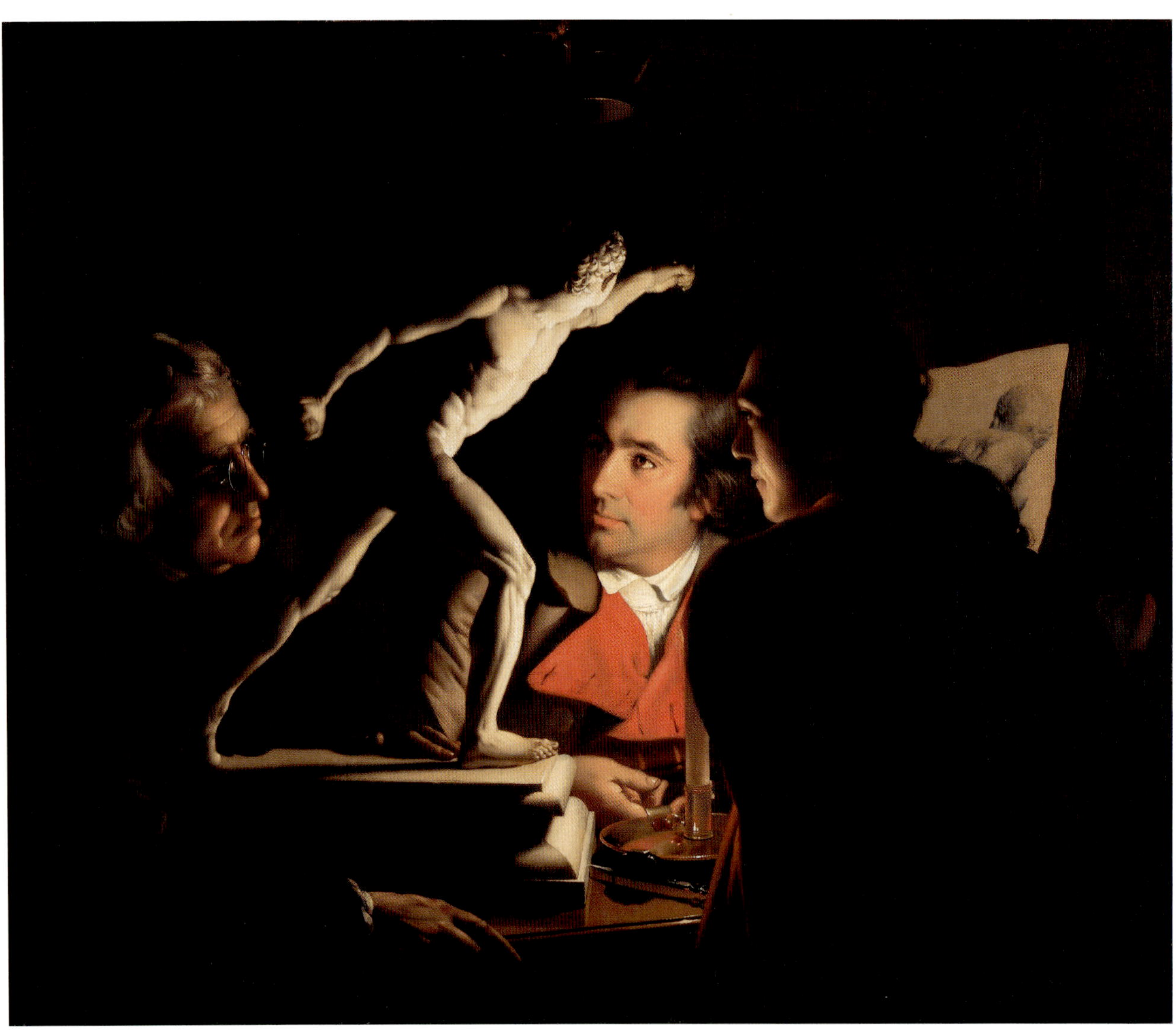

1

Three Persons viewing the Gladiator by Candlelight, 1765
Oil on canvas, 102.5 × 122 cm
Private collection

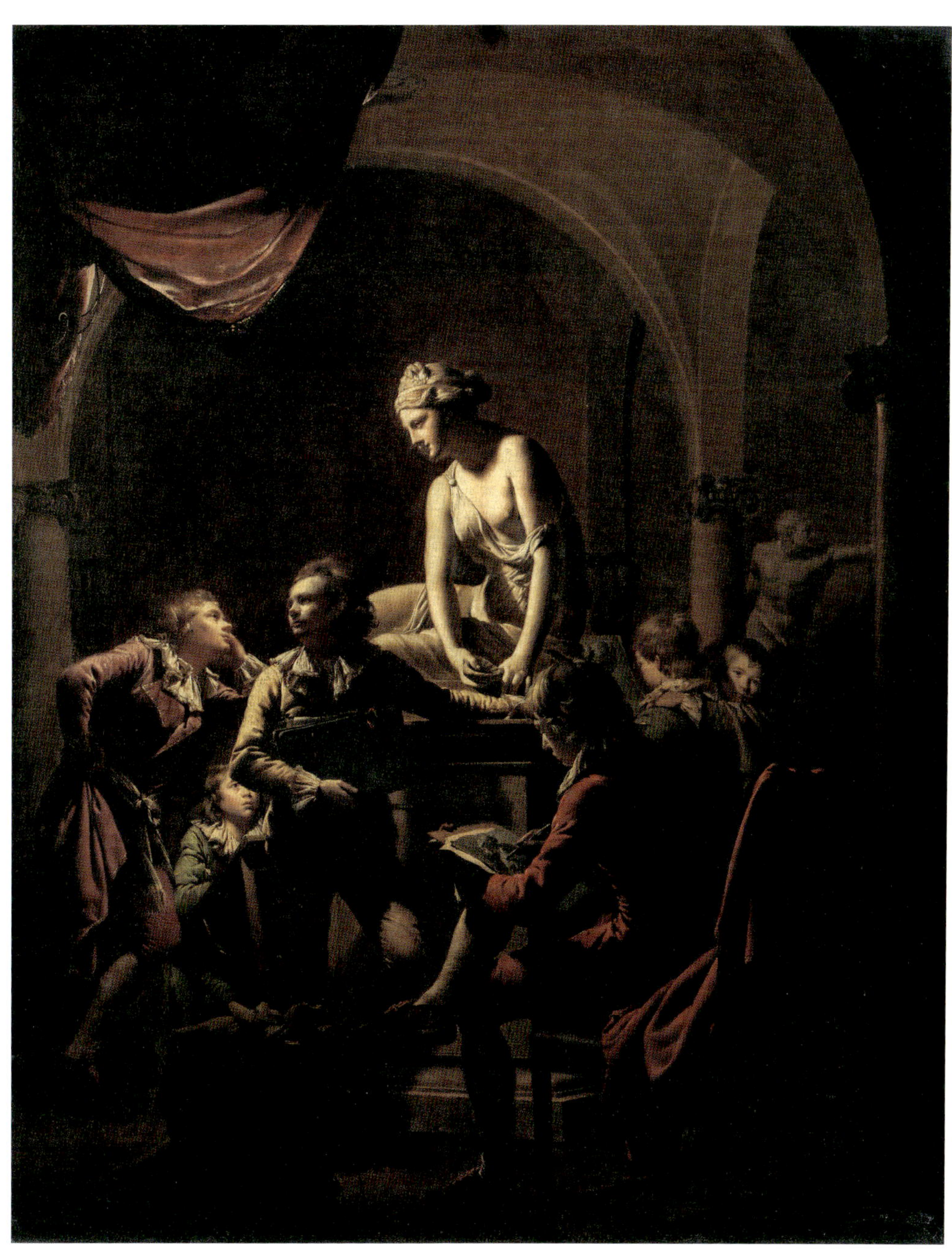

2

An Academy by Lamplight, 1769
Oil on canvas, 127 × 101 cm
Yale Center for British Art, Paul Mellon Collection

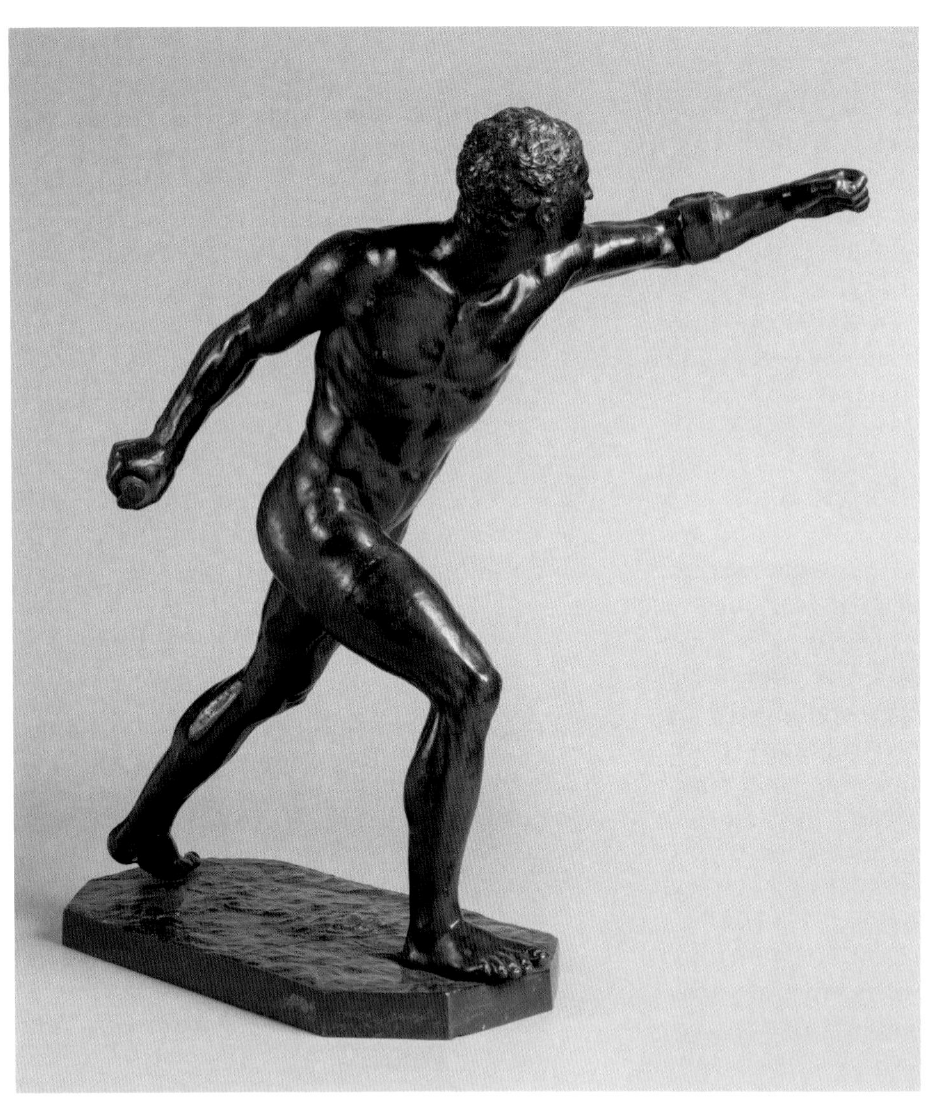

3

Unknown
Borghese Gladiator, about 1775–about 1899
Bronze, 51 × 38 cm
National Trust Collections, Shugborough (The Anson Collection)

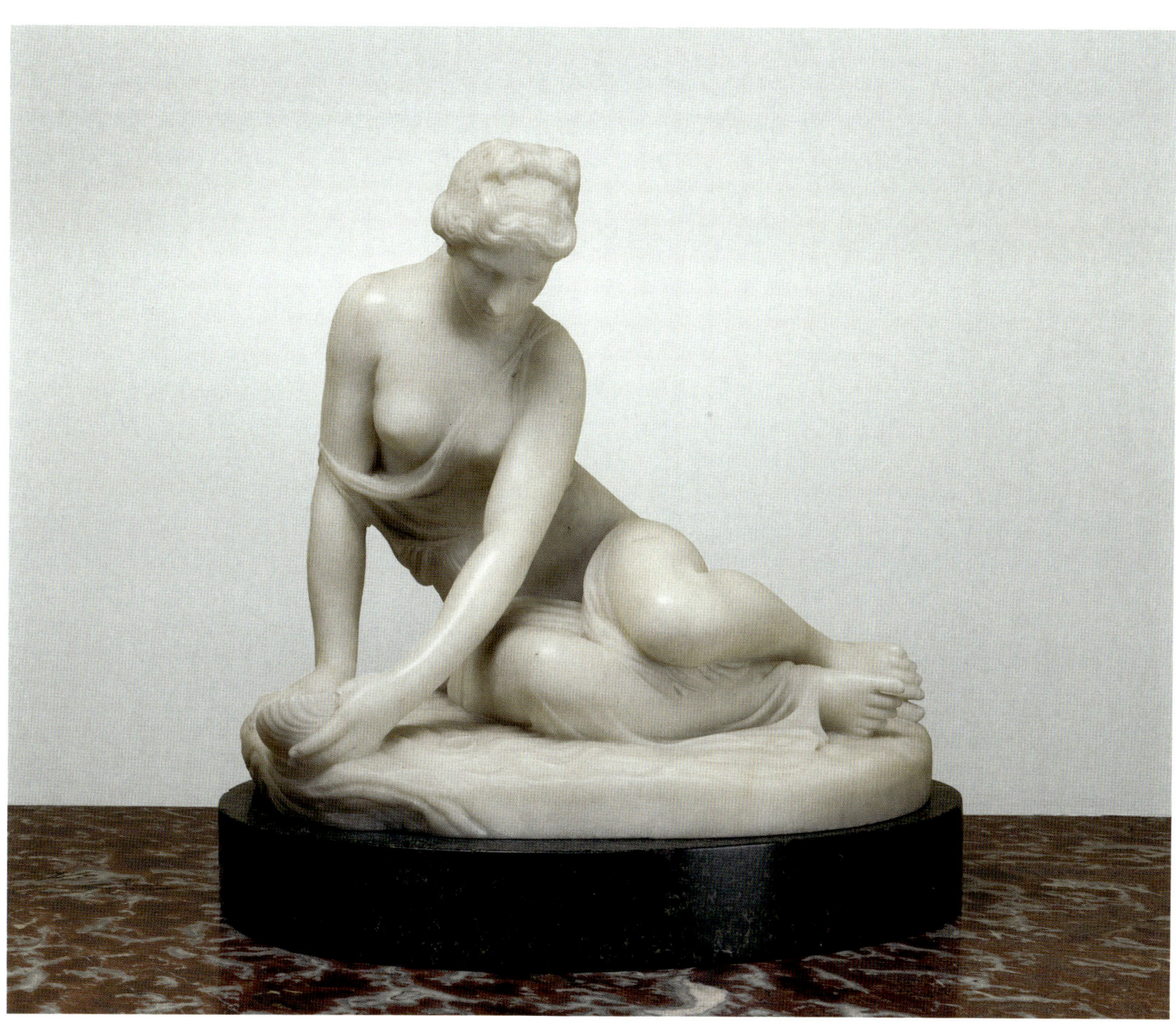

4

Lorenzo Bartolini after Antoine Coysevox
Nymph with a Shell, 1822
Carrara marble, 34 × 39 × 39 cm
Trustees of the Weston Park Foundation

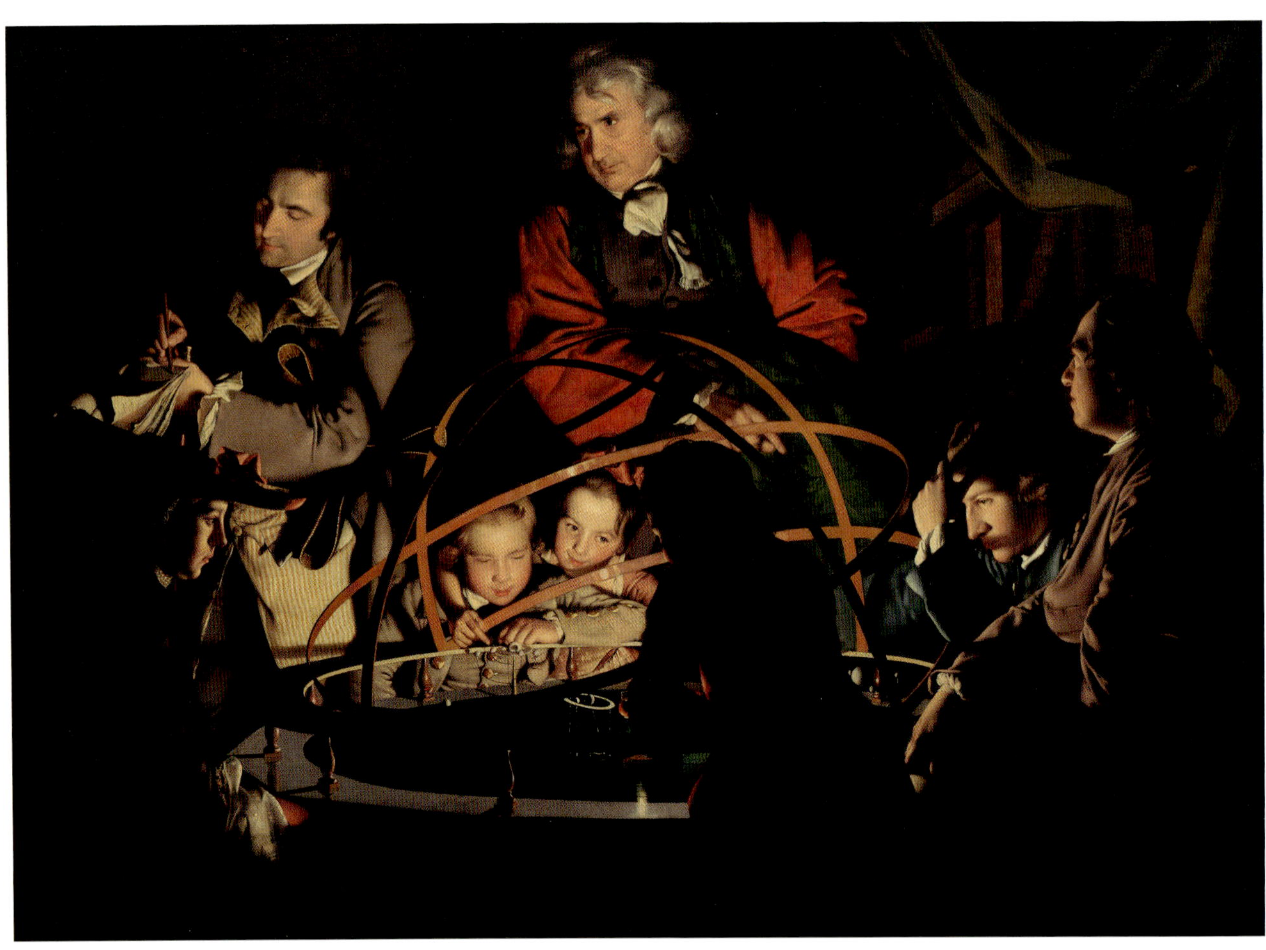

5

A Philosopher giving that Lecture on the Orrery in which a Lamp is put in the Place of the Sun, exhibited 1766
Oil on canvas, 147.3 × 203.2 cm
Derby Museums

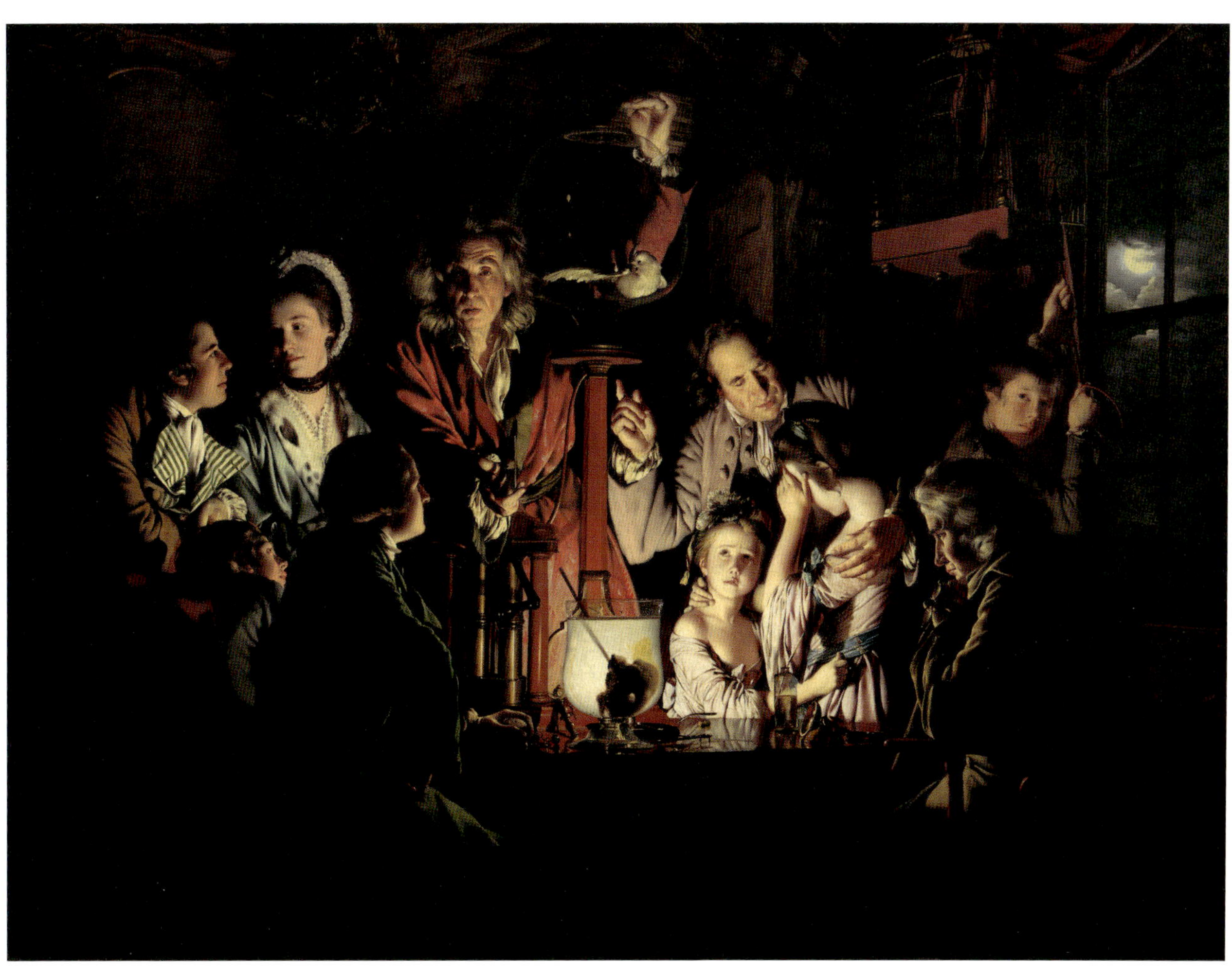

6

An Experiment on a Bird in the Air Pump, 1768
Oil on canvas, 183 × 244 cm
The National Gallery, London

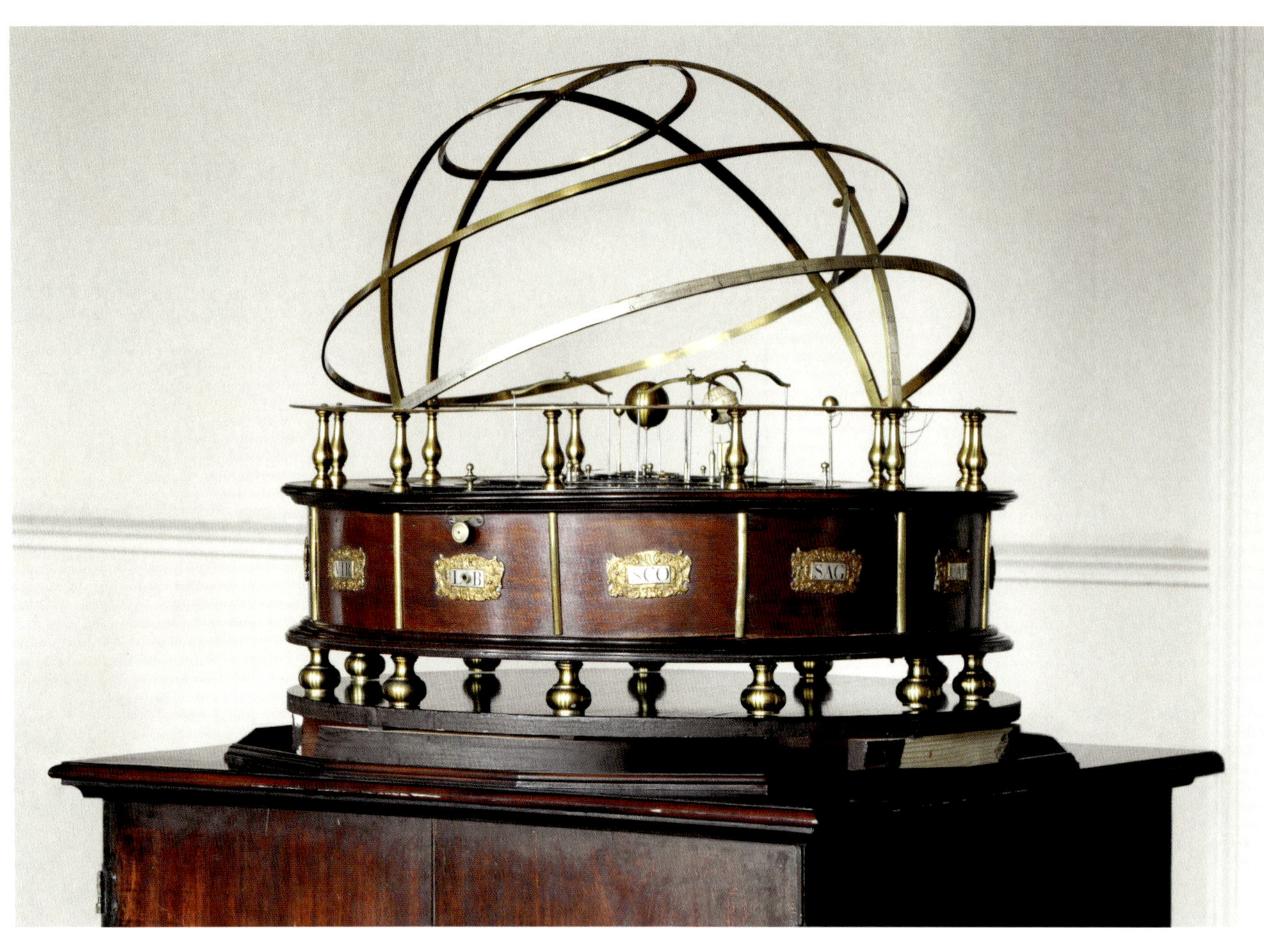

7

Attributed to Benjamin Cole
Grand Orrery, about 1750
Mahogany, brass, steel, ivory and ebony, 63.5 × 76.2 cm
Dumfries House, part of The King's Foundation

8

Nairne & Blunt
Air Pump (Vacuum Fountain), about 1774–93
Glass, metal (brass), wood and ivory, 133 × 40.8 × 66 cm
Whipple Museum of the History of Science, University of Cambridge

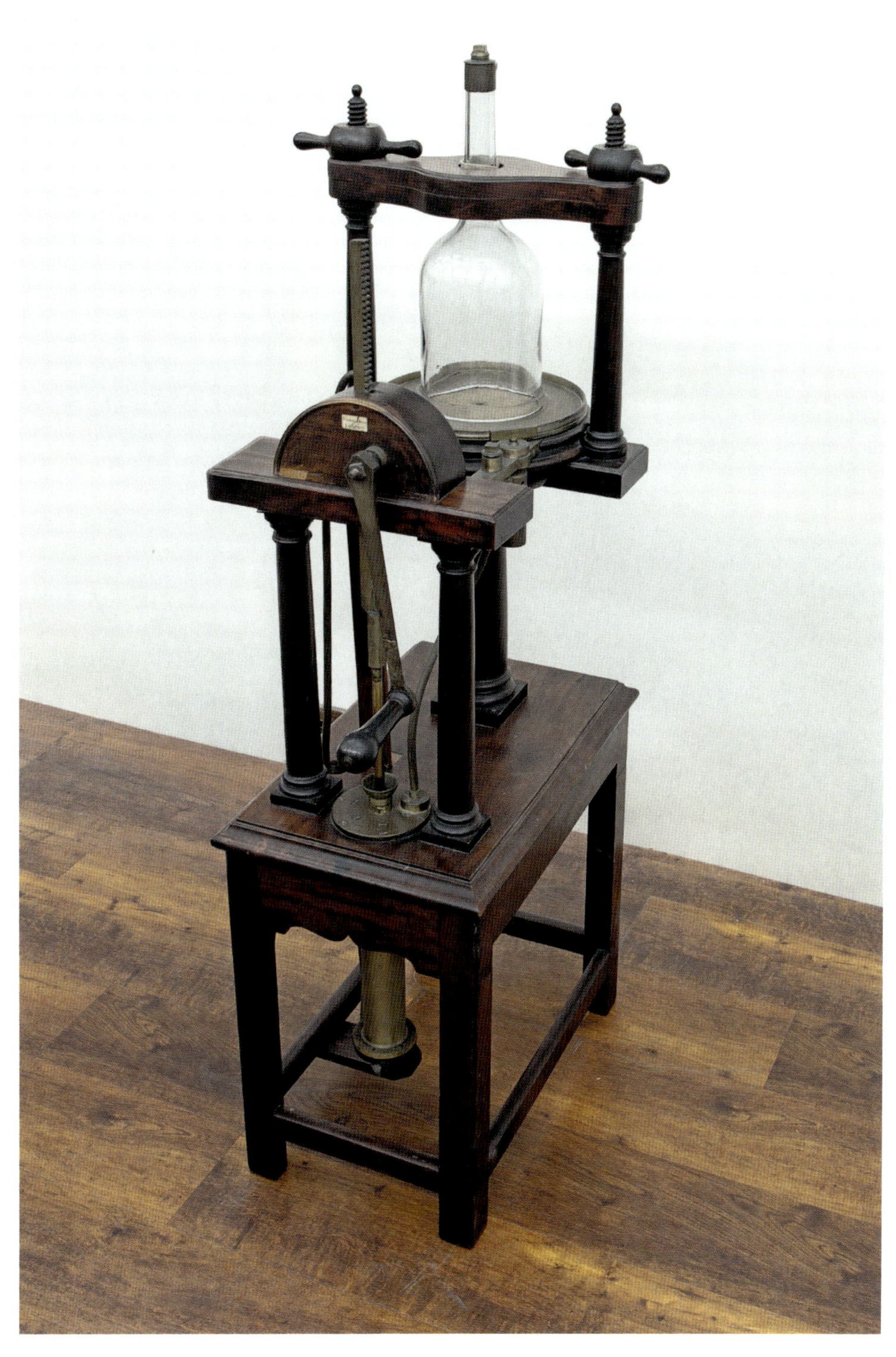

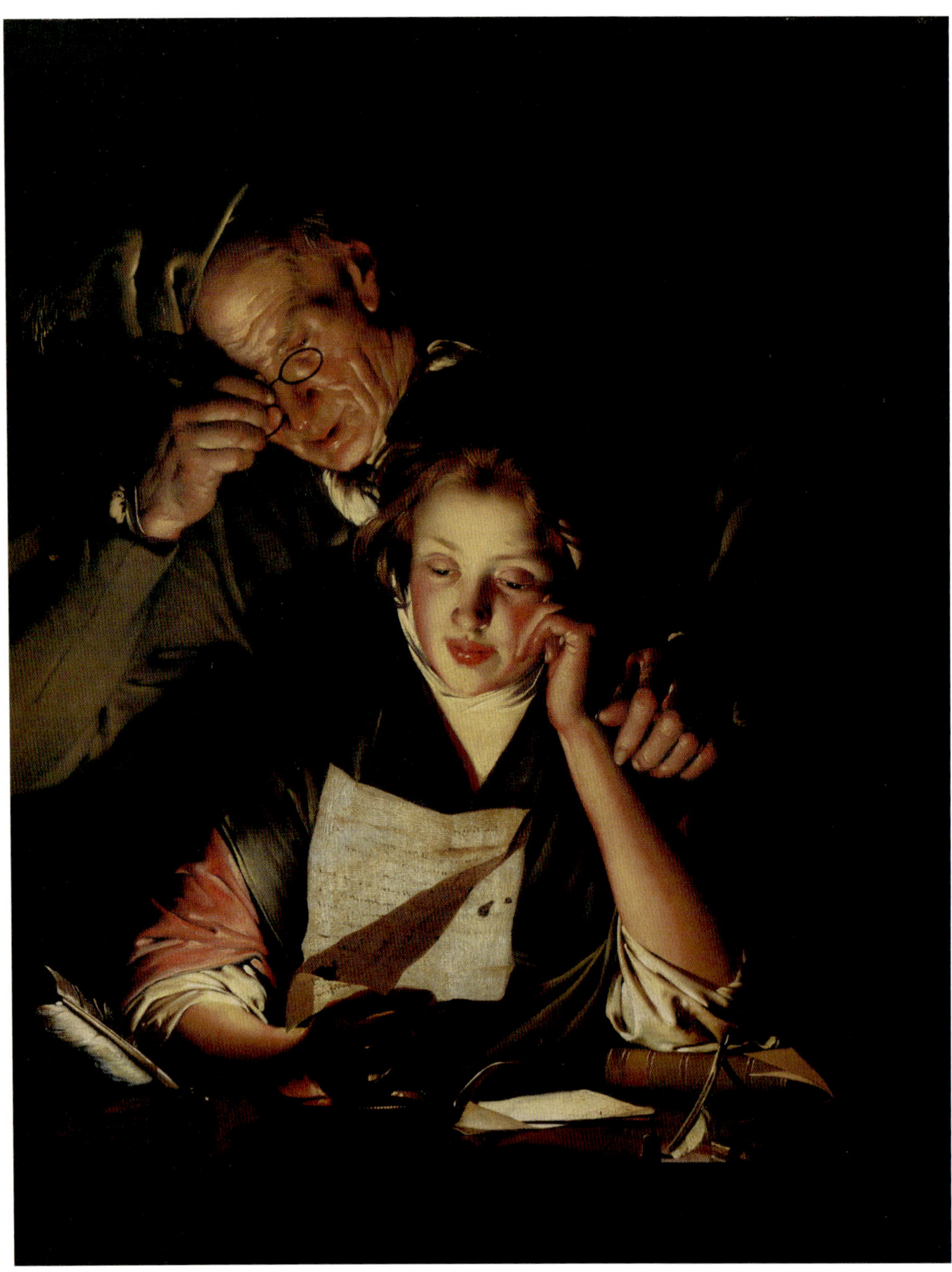

9

A Girl reading a Letter with an Old Man reading over her Shoulder, about 1767–70
Oil on canvas, 91.5 × 71.2 cm
Private collection, c/o Omnia Art

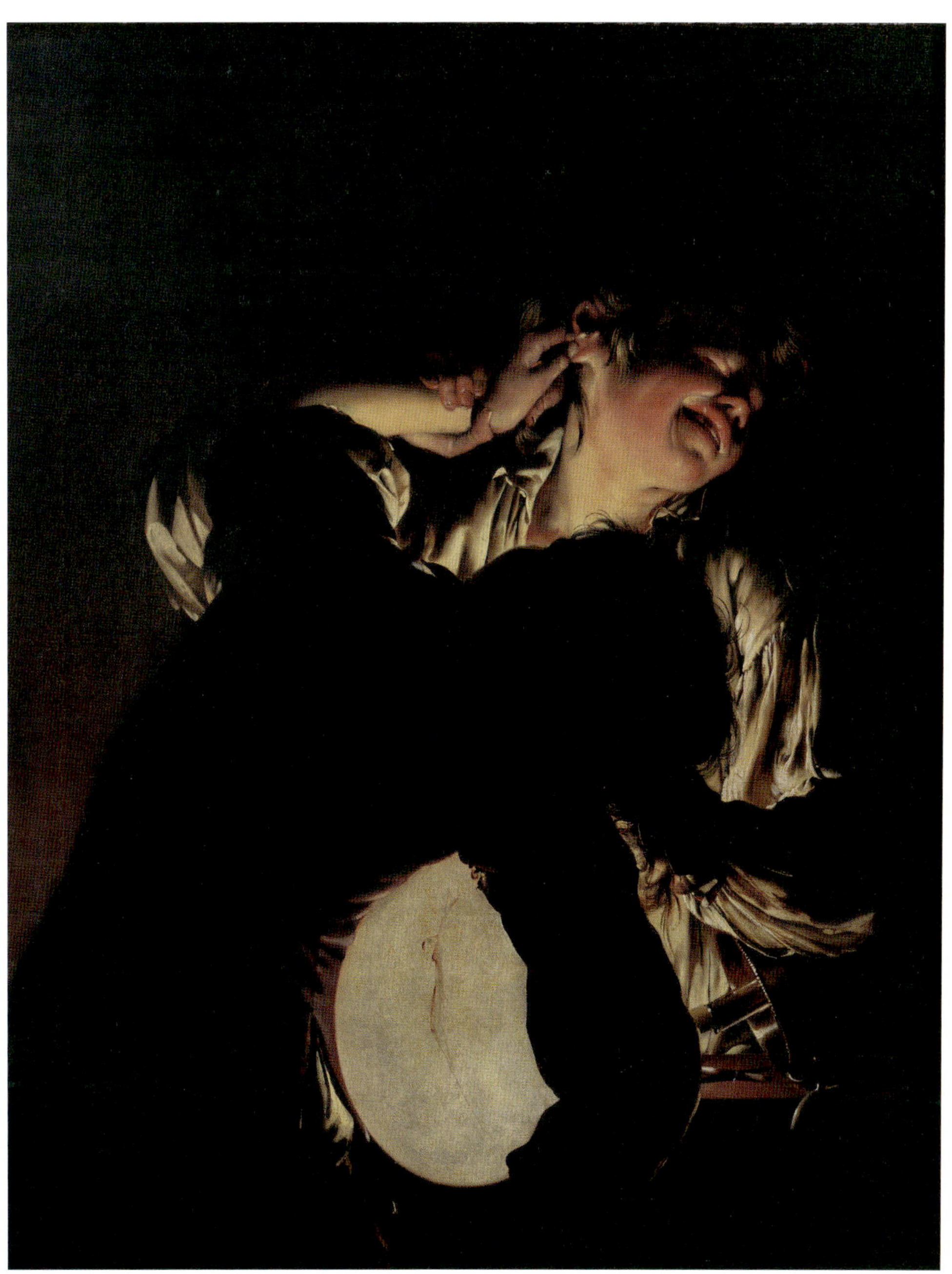

10

Two Boys fighting over a Bladder, about 1767–70
Oil on canvas, 91.5 × 71.2 cm
Private collection, c/o Omnia Art

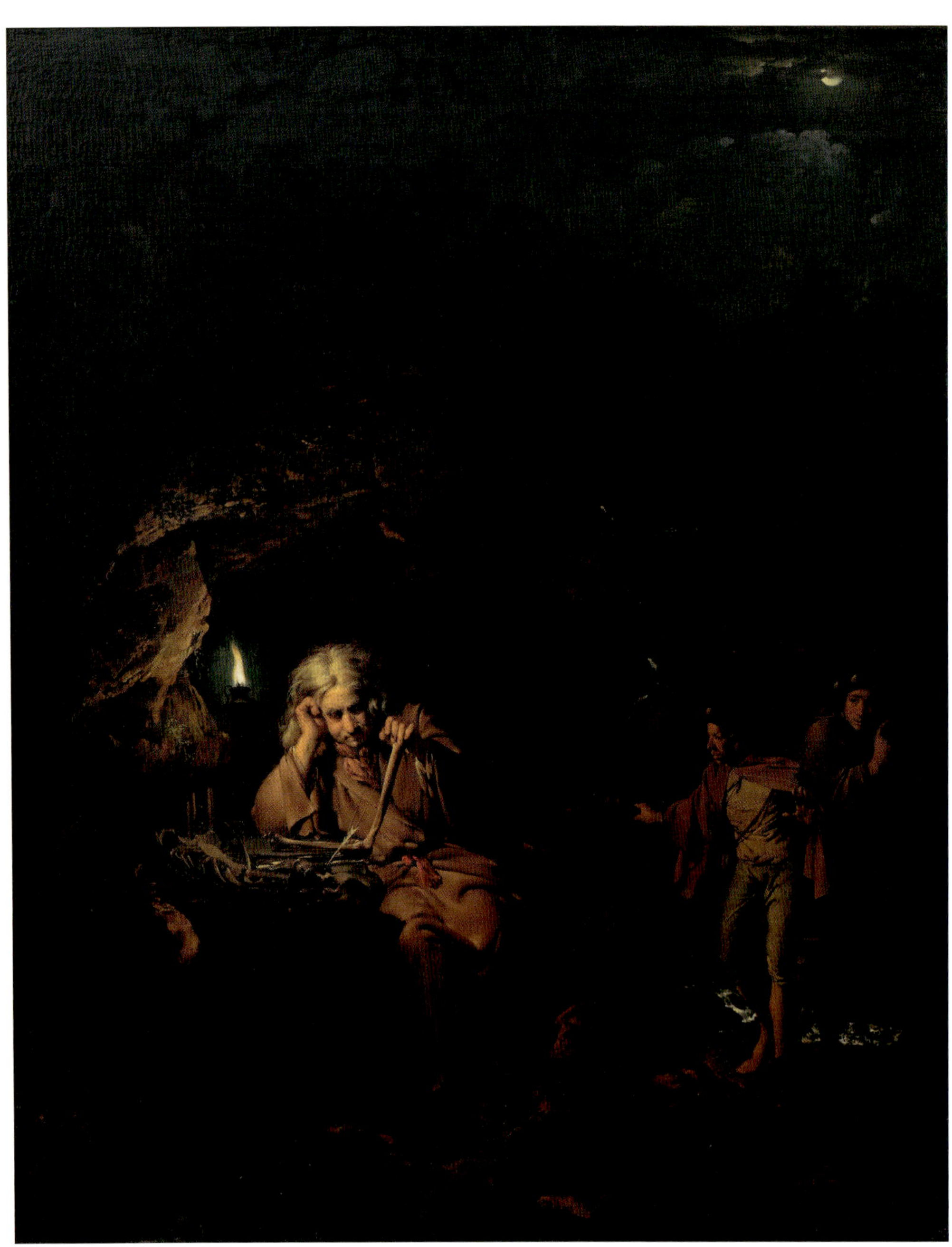

11

A Philosopher by Lamplight, about 1769
Oil on canvas, 128.2 × 101.6 cm
Derby Museums

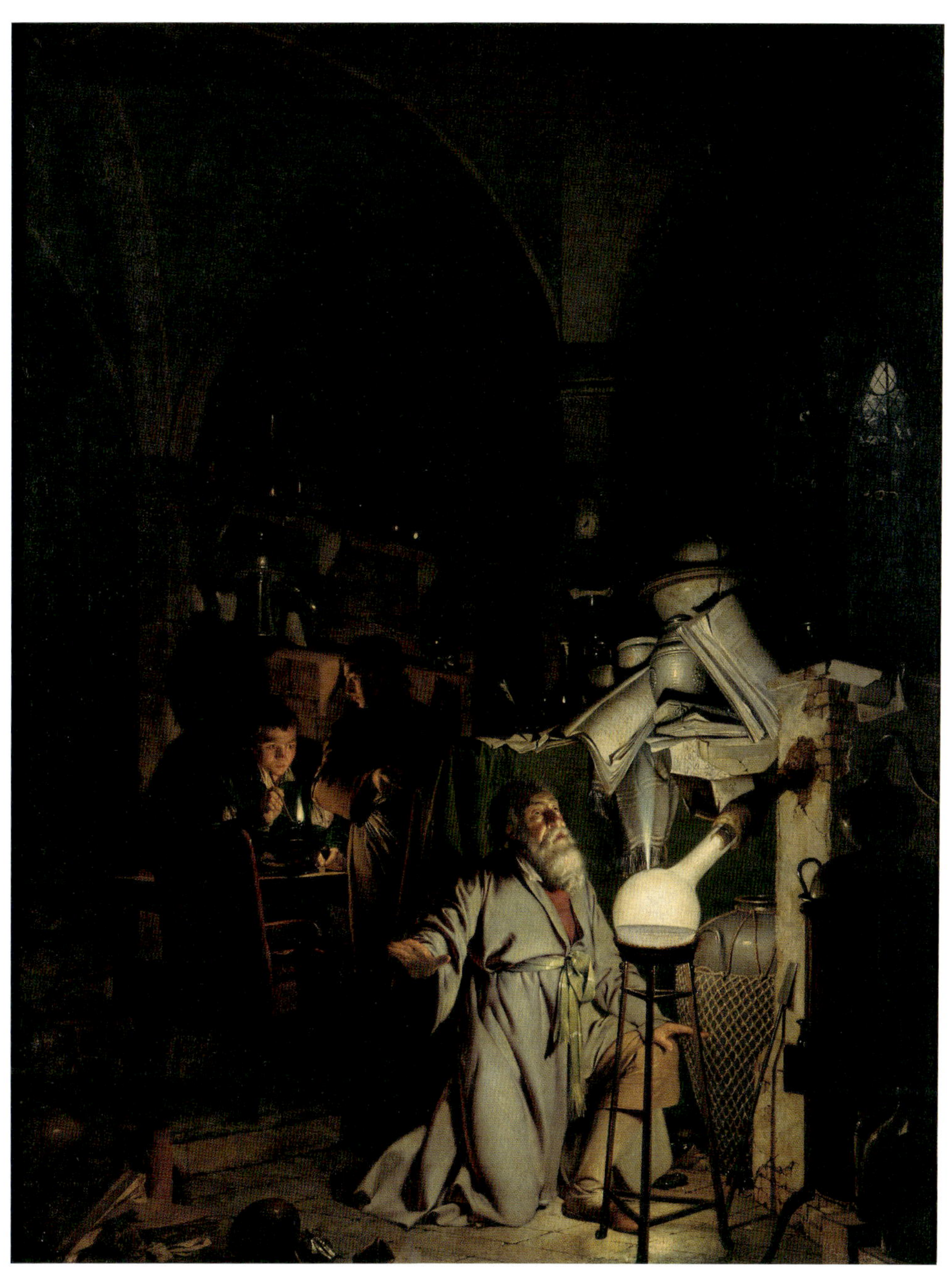

12

The Alchymist in Search of the Philosopher's Stone, discovers Phosphorus, and prays for the Successful Conclusion of his Operation, as was the Custom of the Ancient Chymical Astrologers, exhibited 1771, reworked and dated 1795
Oil on canvas, 127 × 101.6 cm
Derby Museums

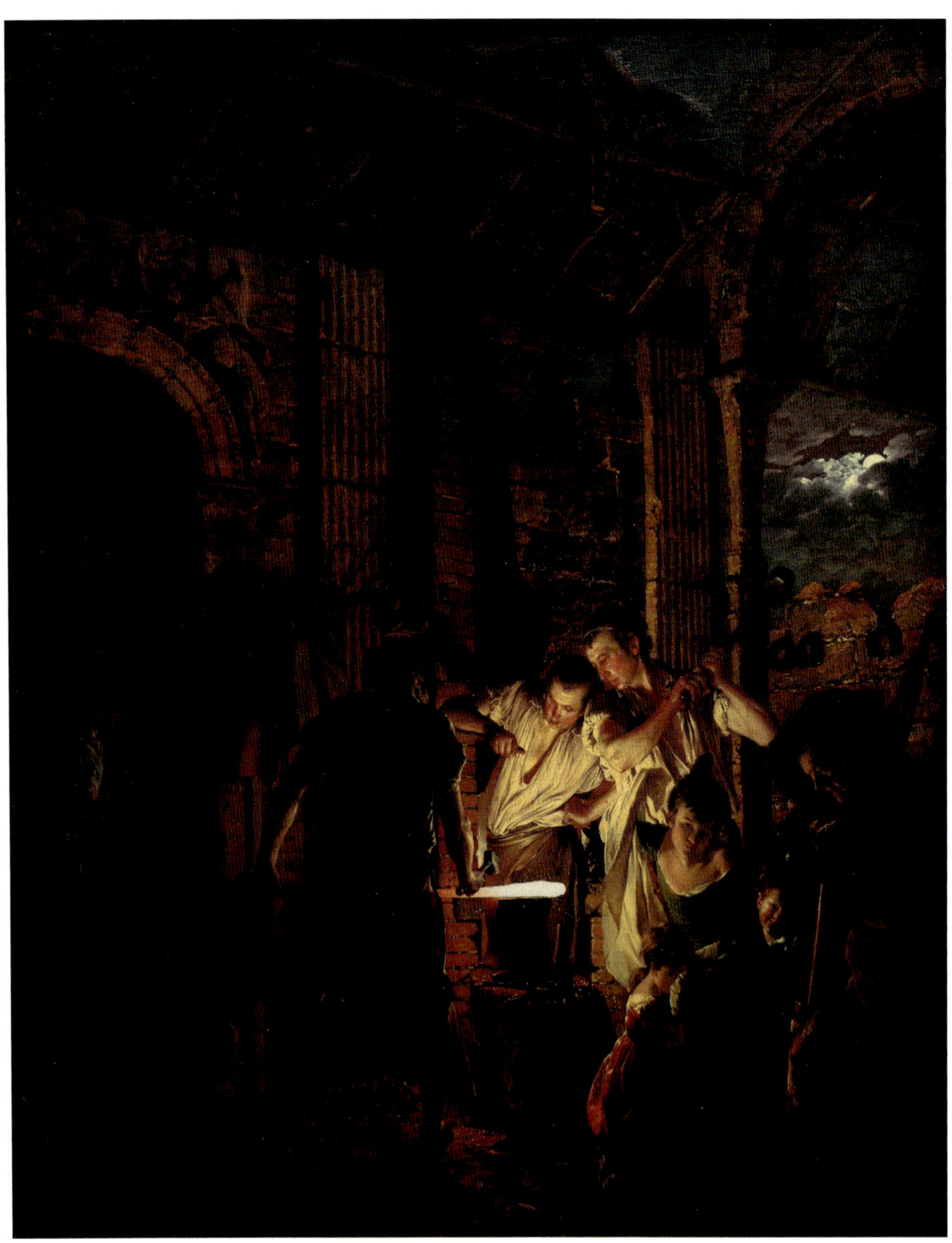

13

A Blacksmith's Shop, 1771
Oil on canvas, 125.7 × 99 cm
Derby Museums

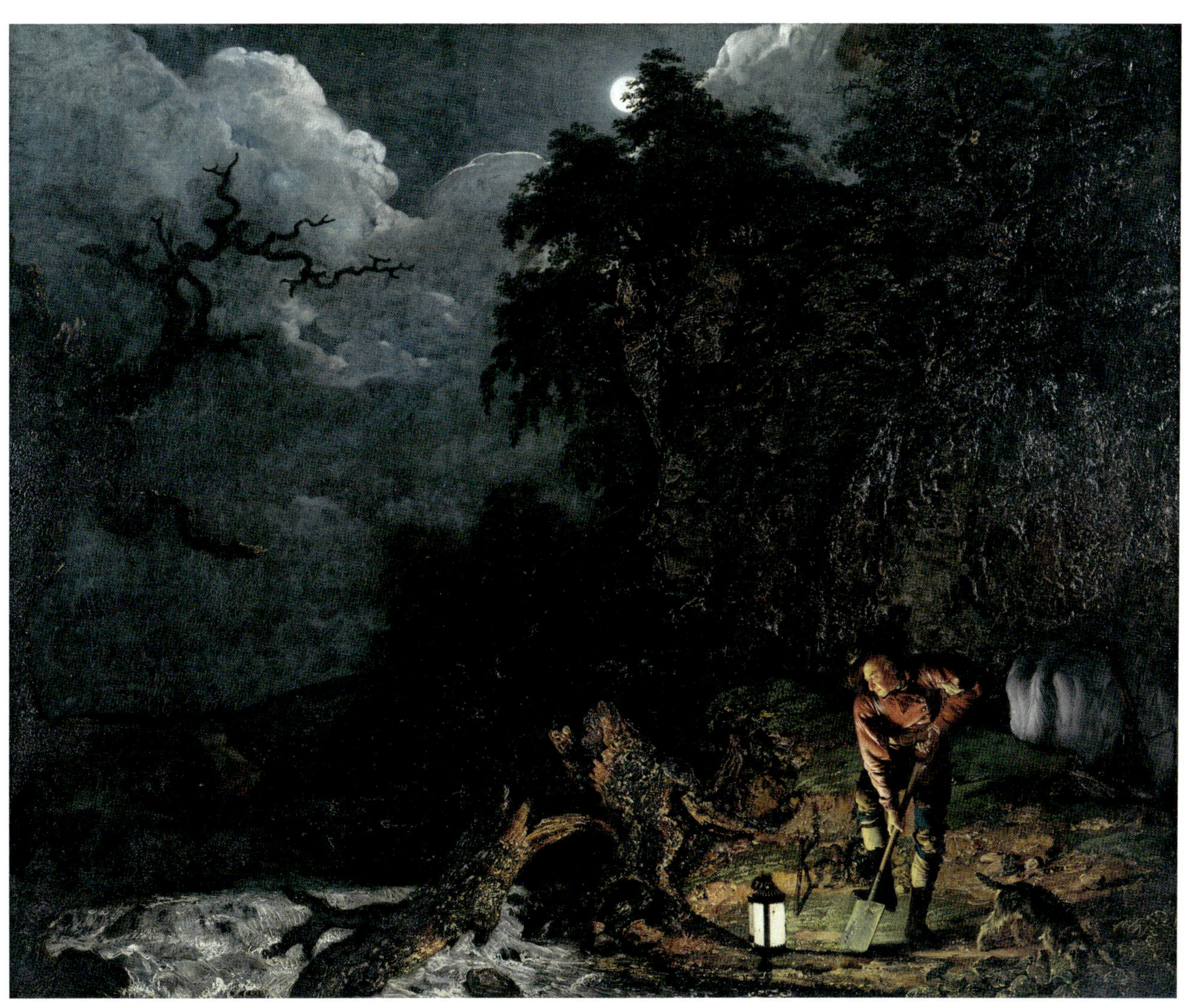

14

An Earthstopper on the Banks of the Derwent, 1773
Oil on canvas, 96.5 × 120.6 cm
Derby Museums

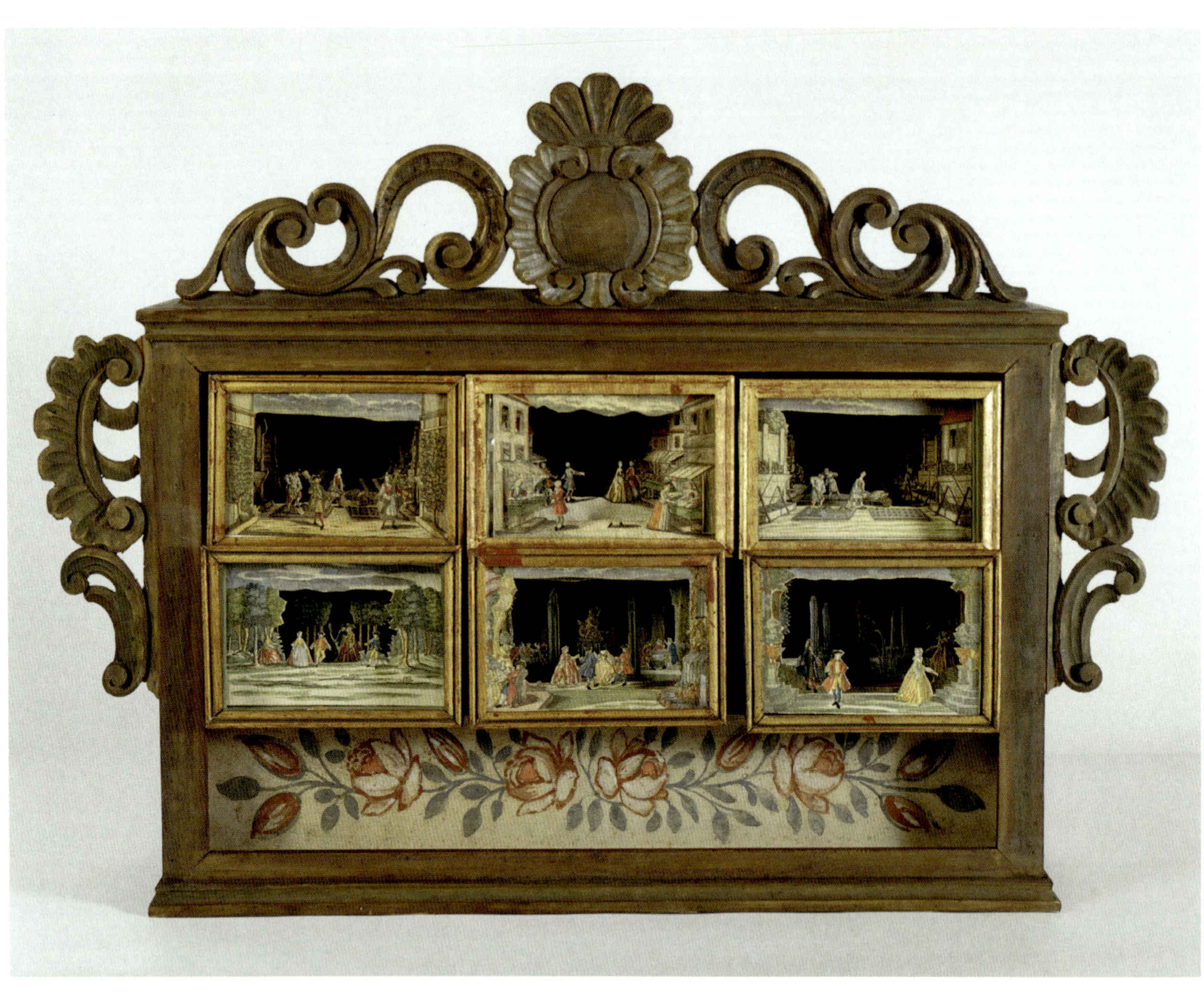

15

Martin Engelbrecht
Peepshow, Toy Theatre, 1721 (probably)
Wood and engraved paper, 51.5 × 71 × 17 cm
Young V&A

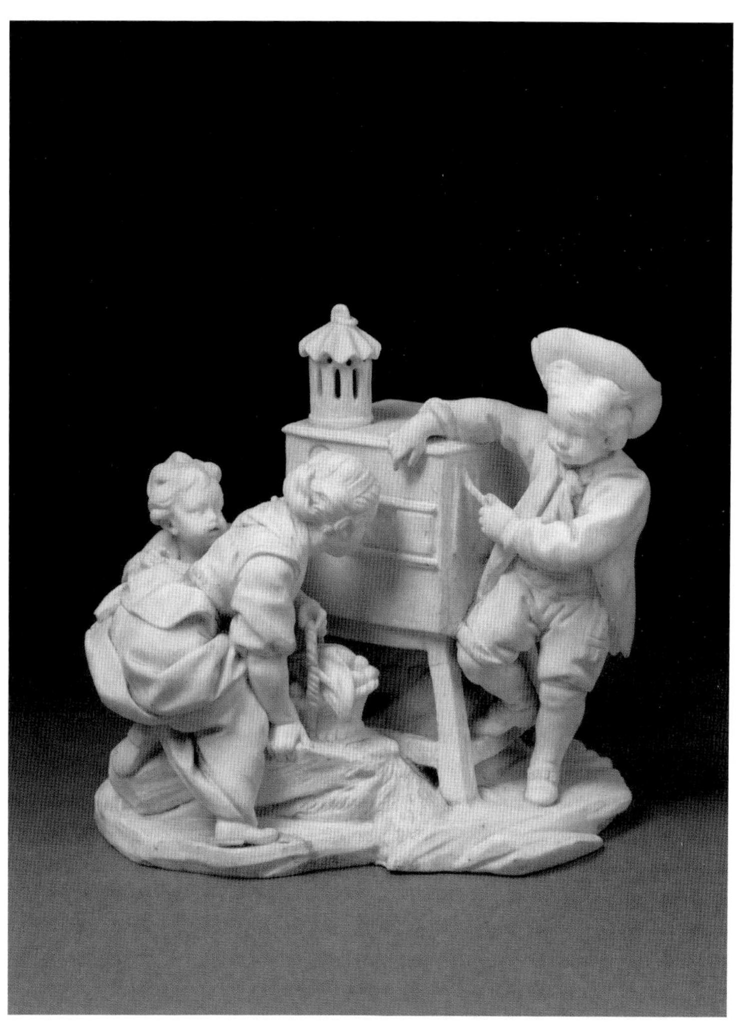

16

Étienne-Maurice Falconet
La Lanterne Magique, about 1757
Biscuit porcelain, Sèvres porcelain factory, 15.6 × 16.5 cm
Victoria and Albert Museum

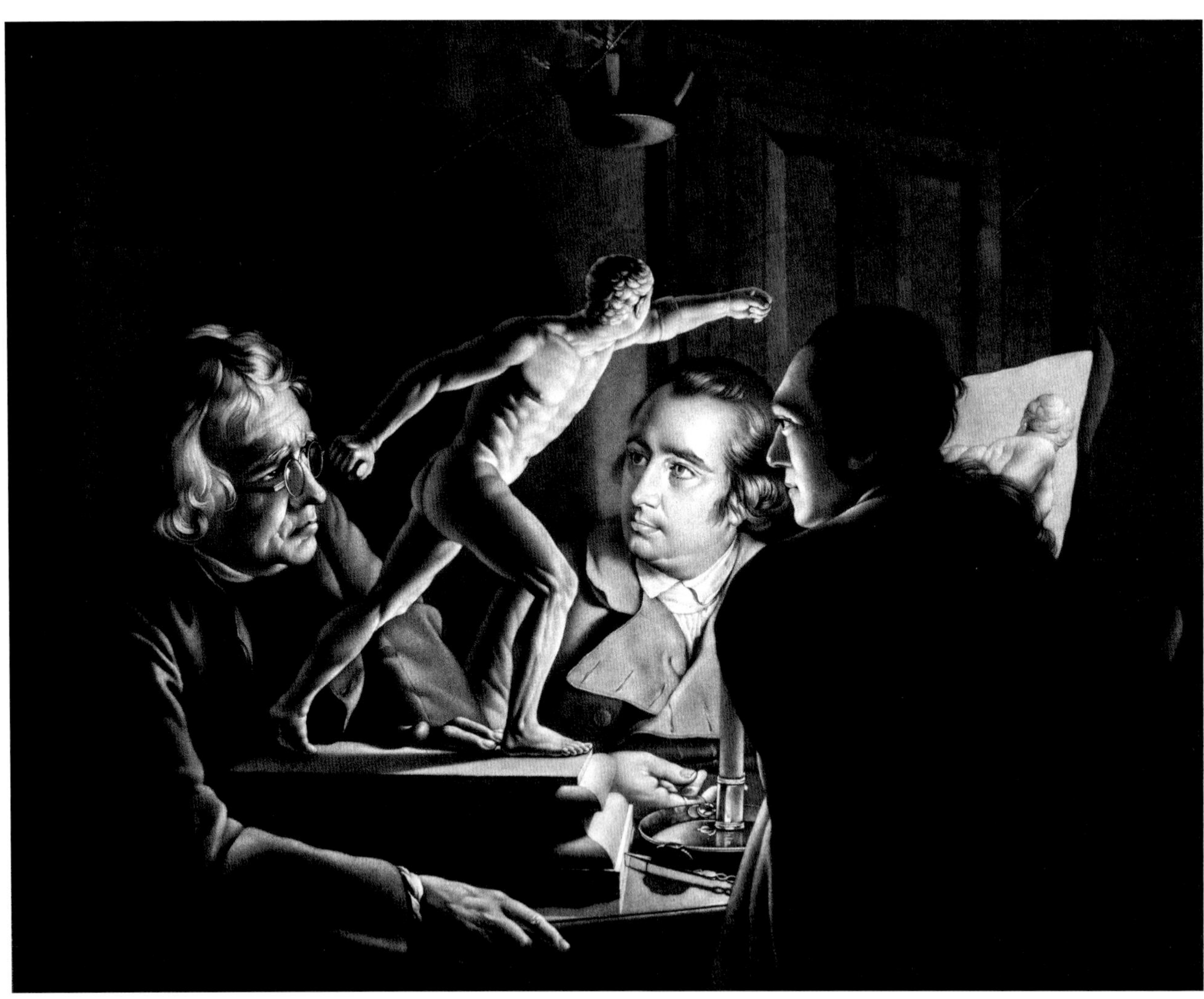

17

William Pether after Joseph Wright of Derby
Three Persons viewing the Gladiator by Candlelight, 1769
Mezzotint, 47 × 57 cm
Derby Museums

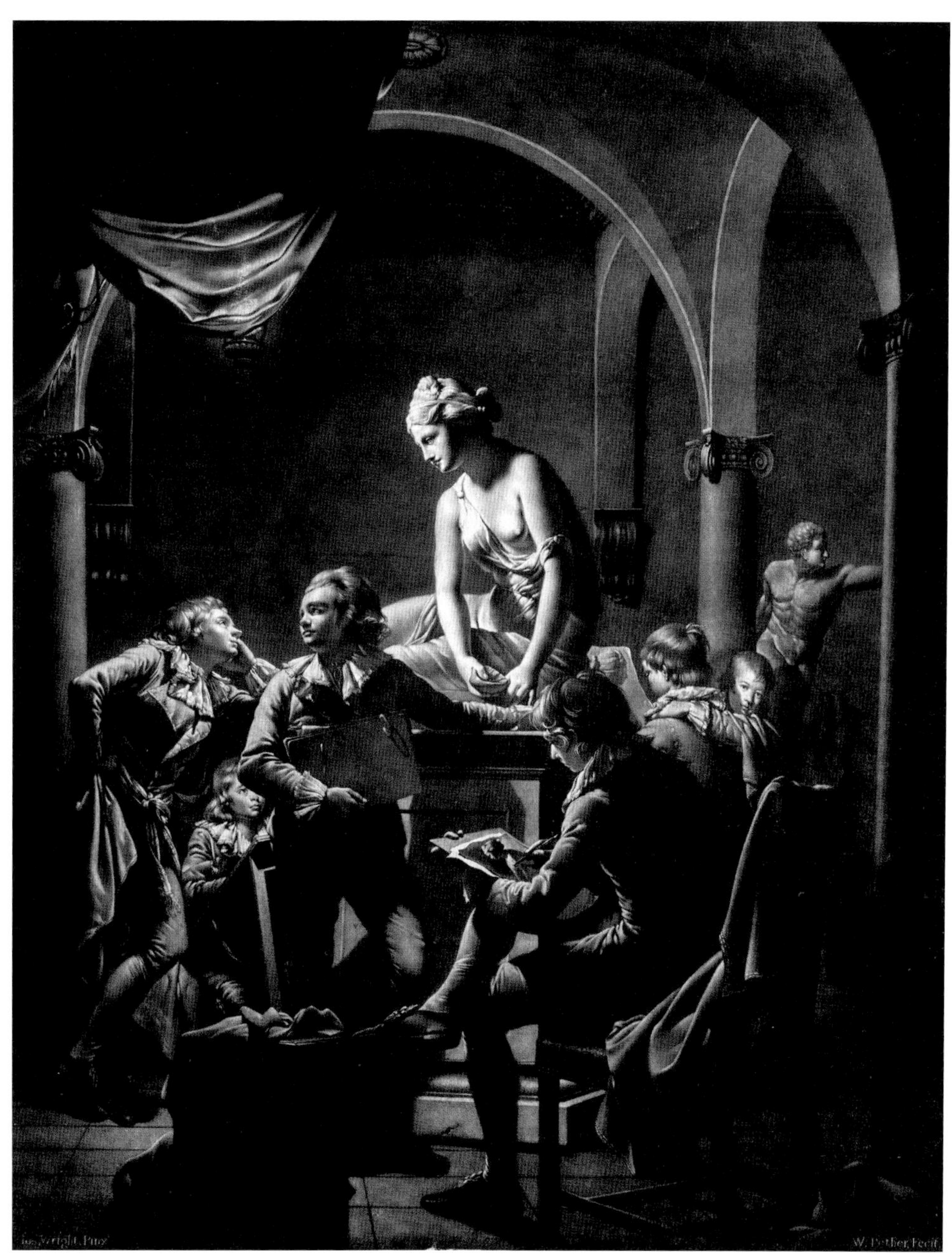

18

William Pether after Joseph Wright of Derby
An Academy by Lamplight, 1771
Mezzotint, 58.9 × 46.4 cm
Derby Museums

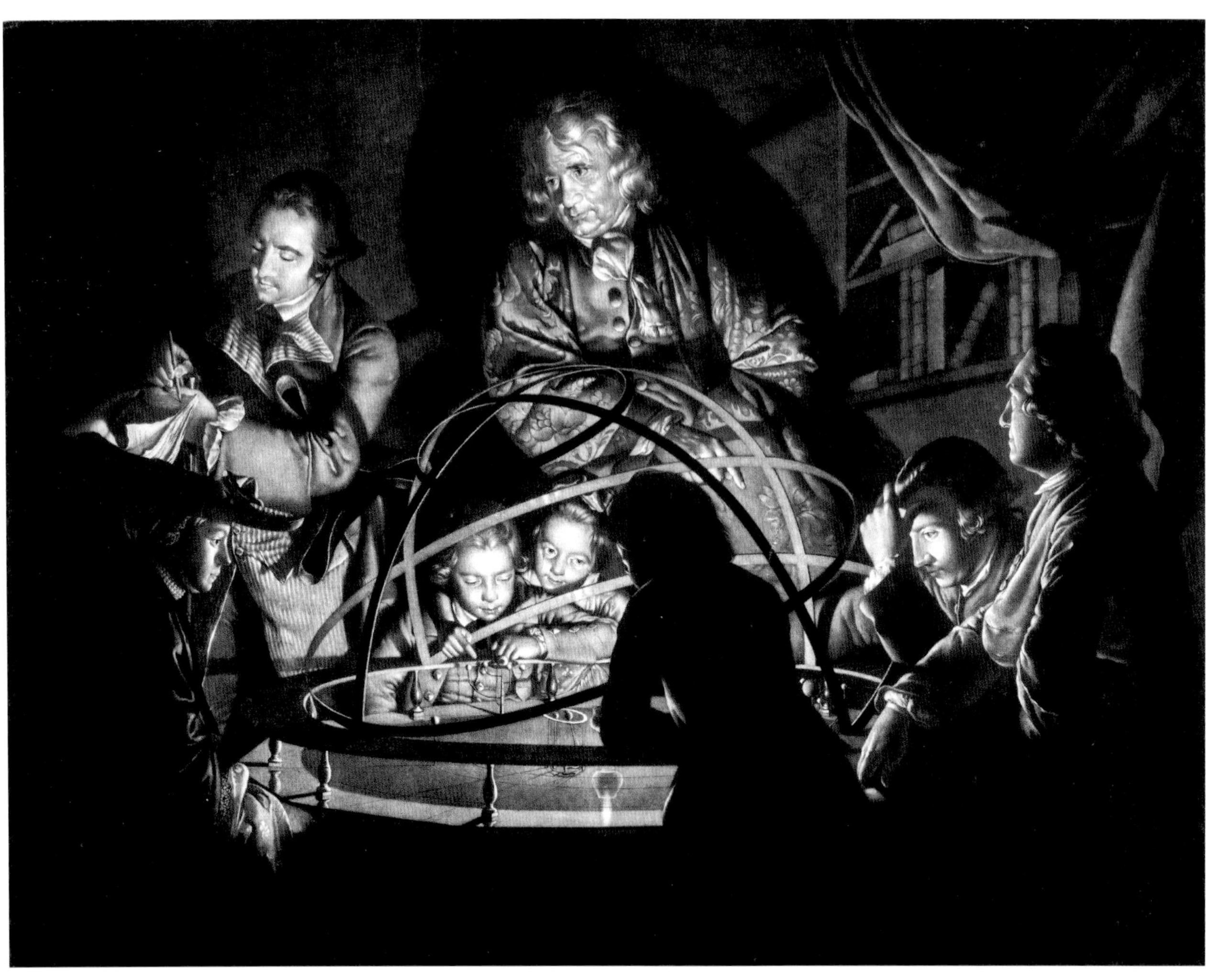

19

William Pether after Joseph Wright of Derby
A Philosopher giving a Lecture on the Orrery, 1768
Mezzotint, 52 × 64.8 cm
Derby Museums

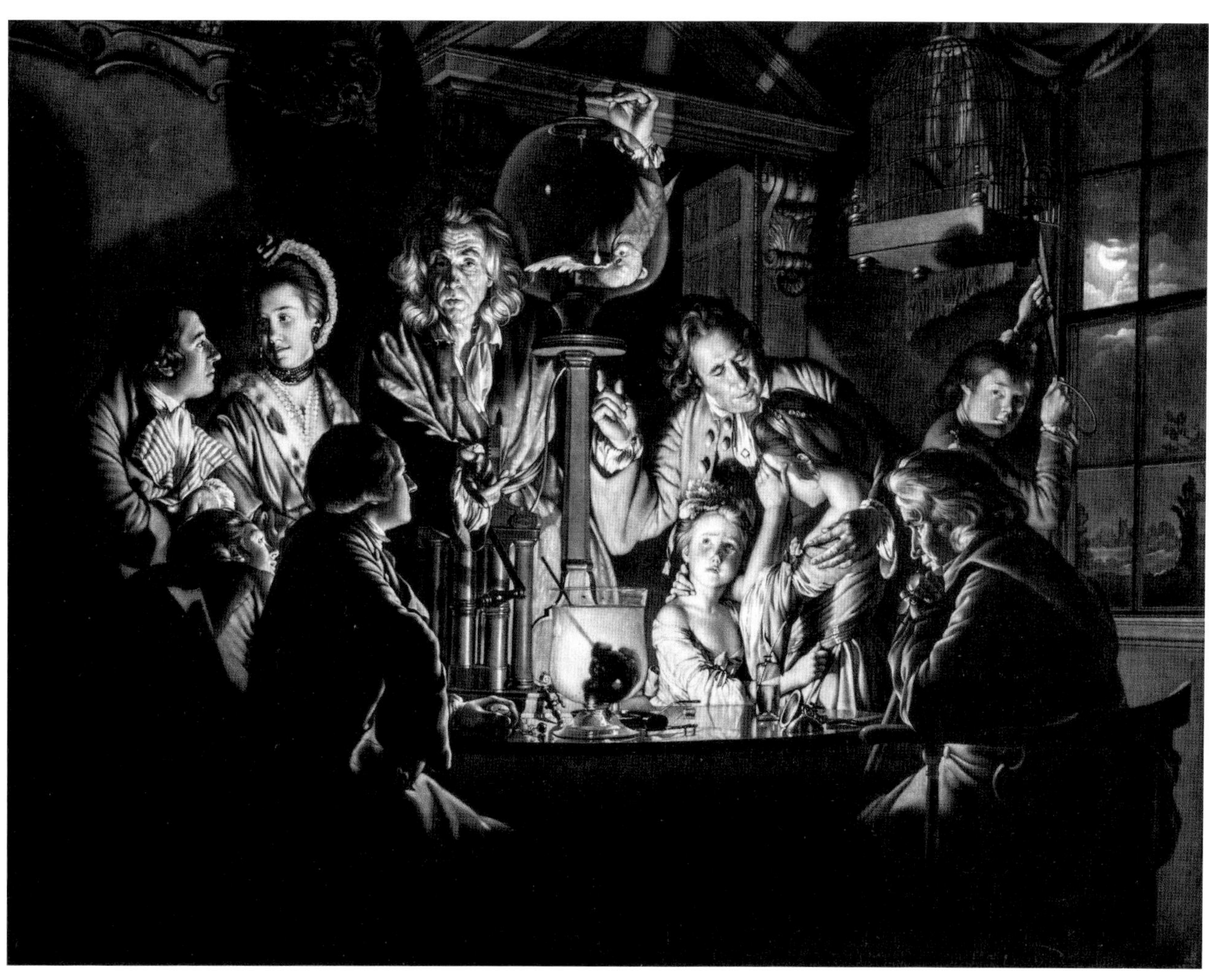

20

Valentine Green after Joseph Wright of Derby
A Philosopher shewing an Experiment on the Air Pump, 1769
Mezzotint, 46.1 × 58.3 cm
Derby Museums

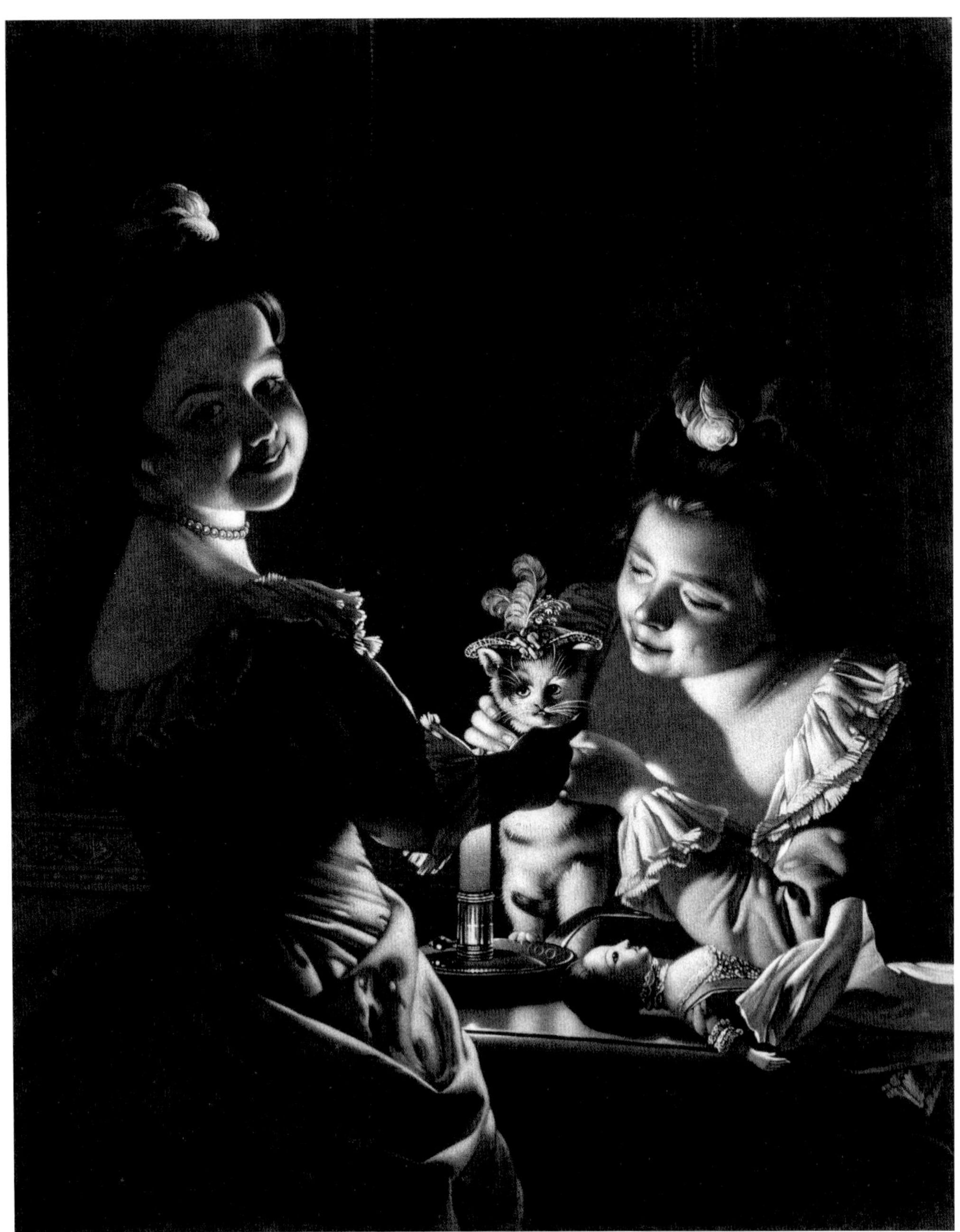

21

Thomas Watson after Joseph Wright of Derby
Miss Kitty dressing, 1781
Mezzotint, 48.6 × 36.5 cm
Derby Museums

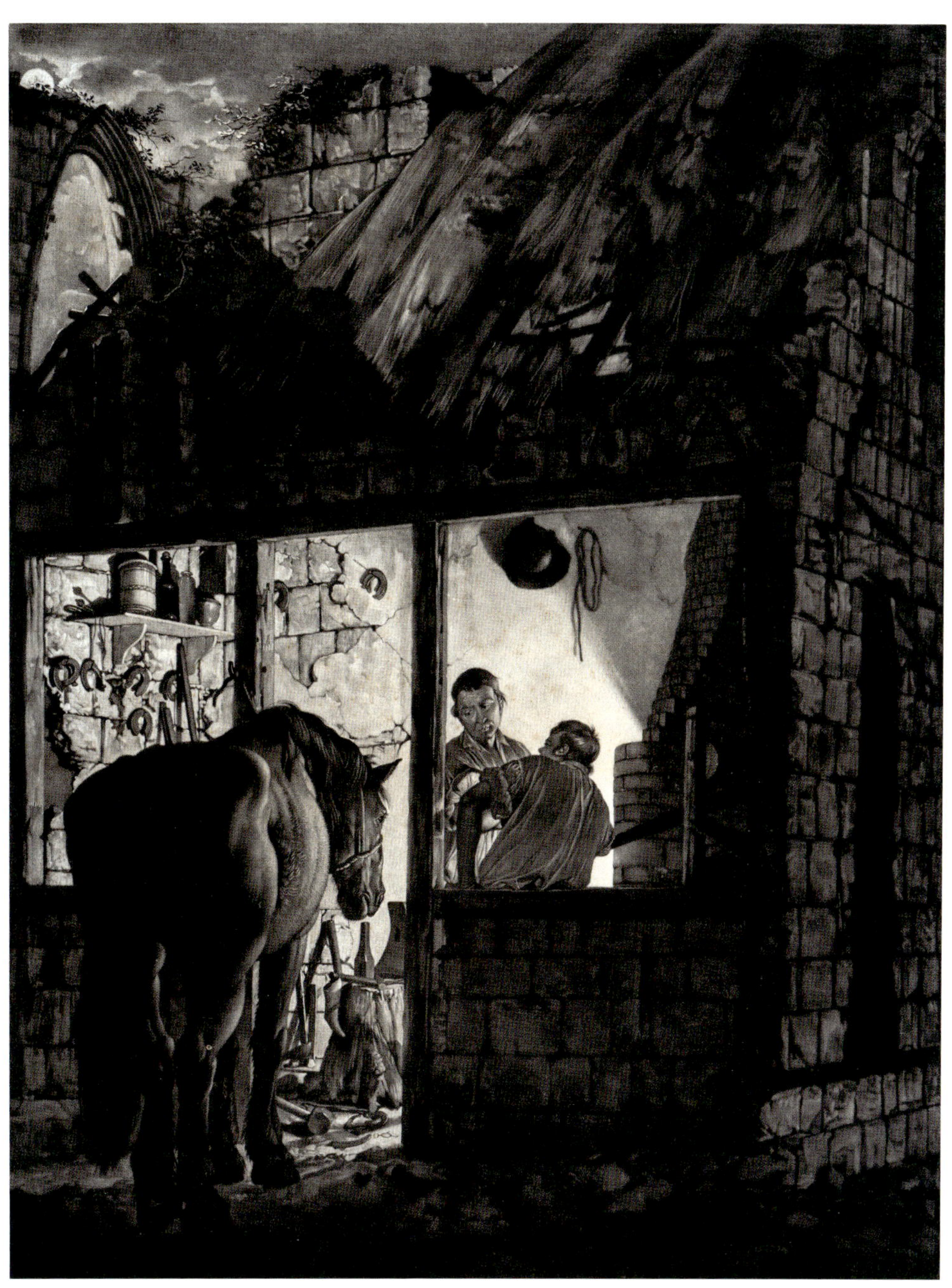

22

William Pether after Joseph Wright of Derby
A Farrier's Shop, 1771
Mezzotint, 53.2 × 38.3 cm
Derby Museums

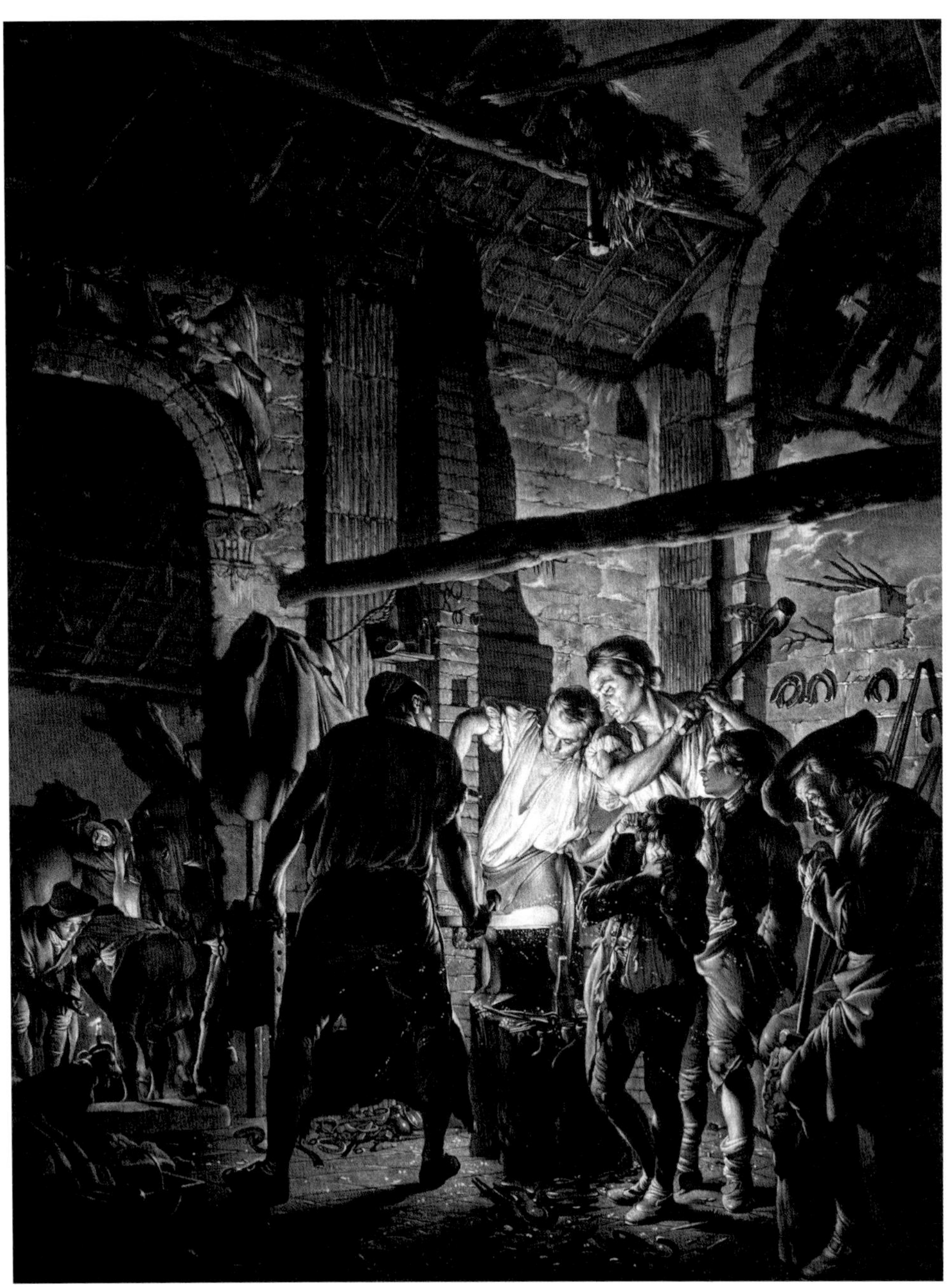

23

Richard Earlom after Joseph Wright of Derby
A Blacksmith's Shop, 1771
Mezzotint, 57.4 × 43.2 cm
Derby Museums

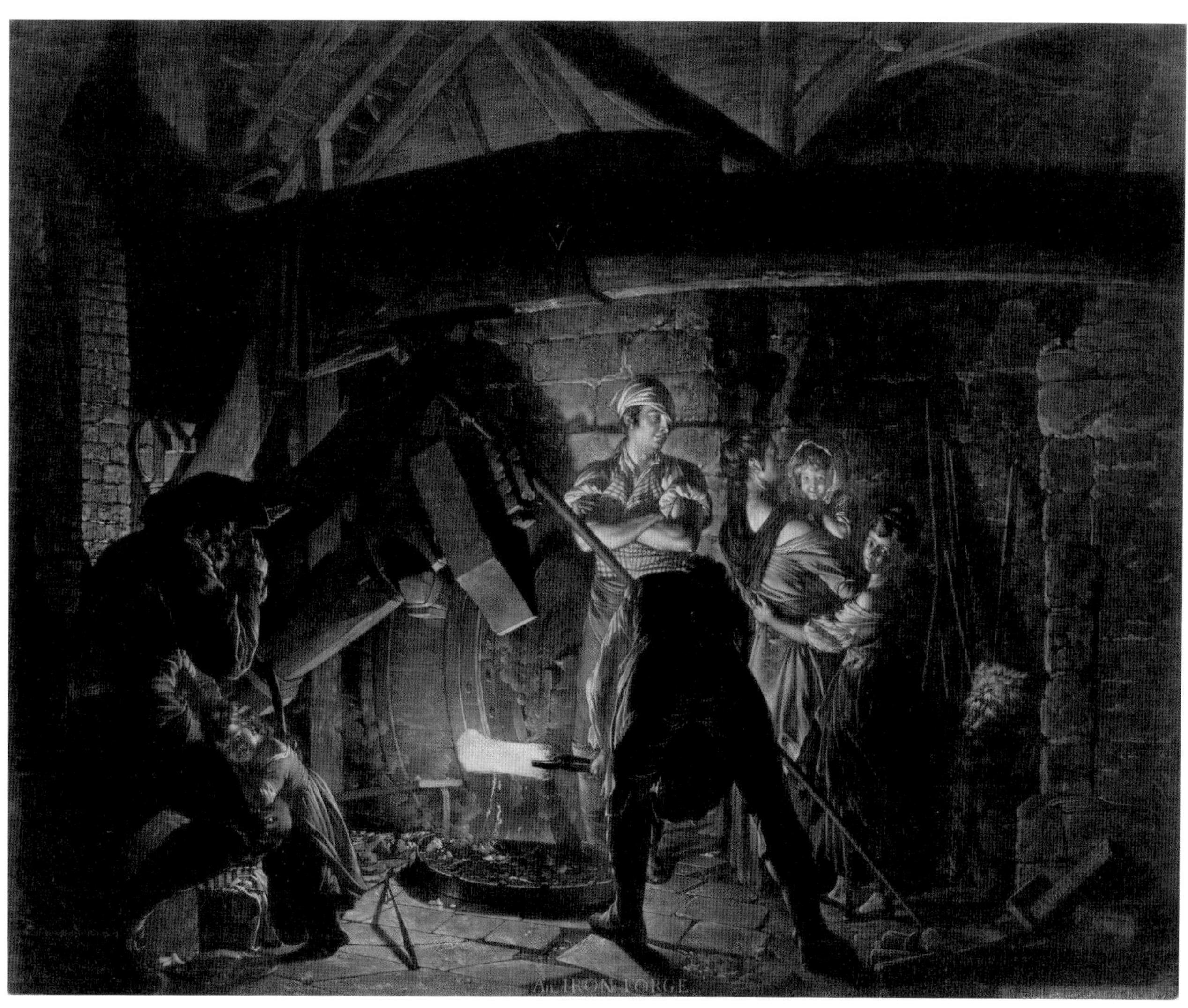

24

Richard Earlom after Joseph Wright of Derby
An Iron Forge, 1773
Mezzotint, 47.8 × 59.2 cm
Derby Museums

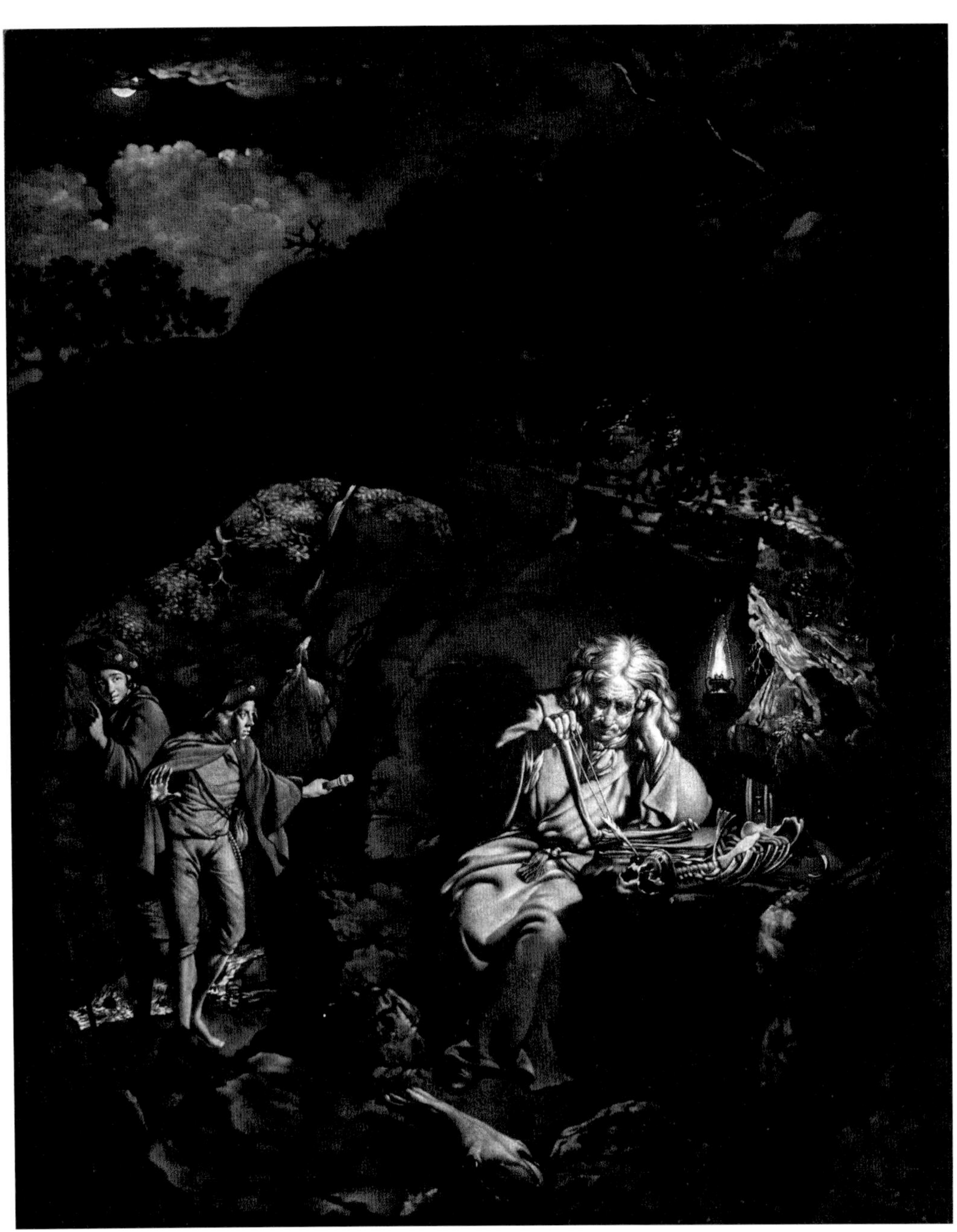

25

William Pether after Joseph Wright of Derby
An Hermit, 1770
Mezzotint, 60.5 × 48 cm
Derby Museums

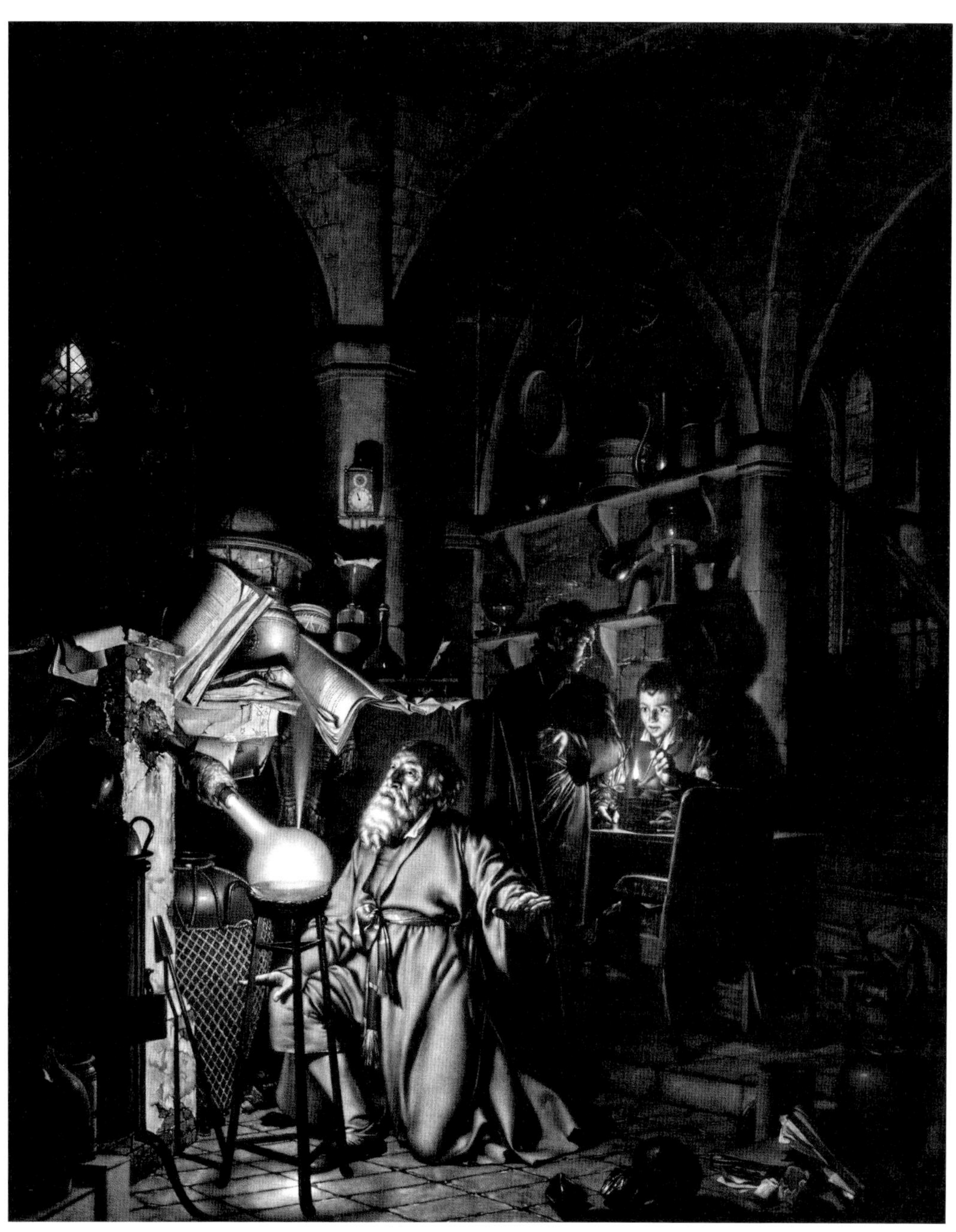

26

William Pether after Joseph Wright of Derby
An Alchymist, 1775
Mezzotint, 62.5 × 50 cm
Derby Museums

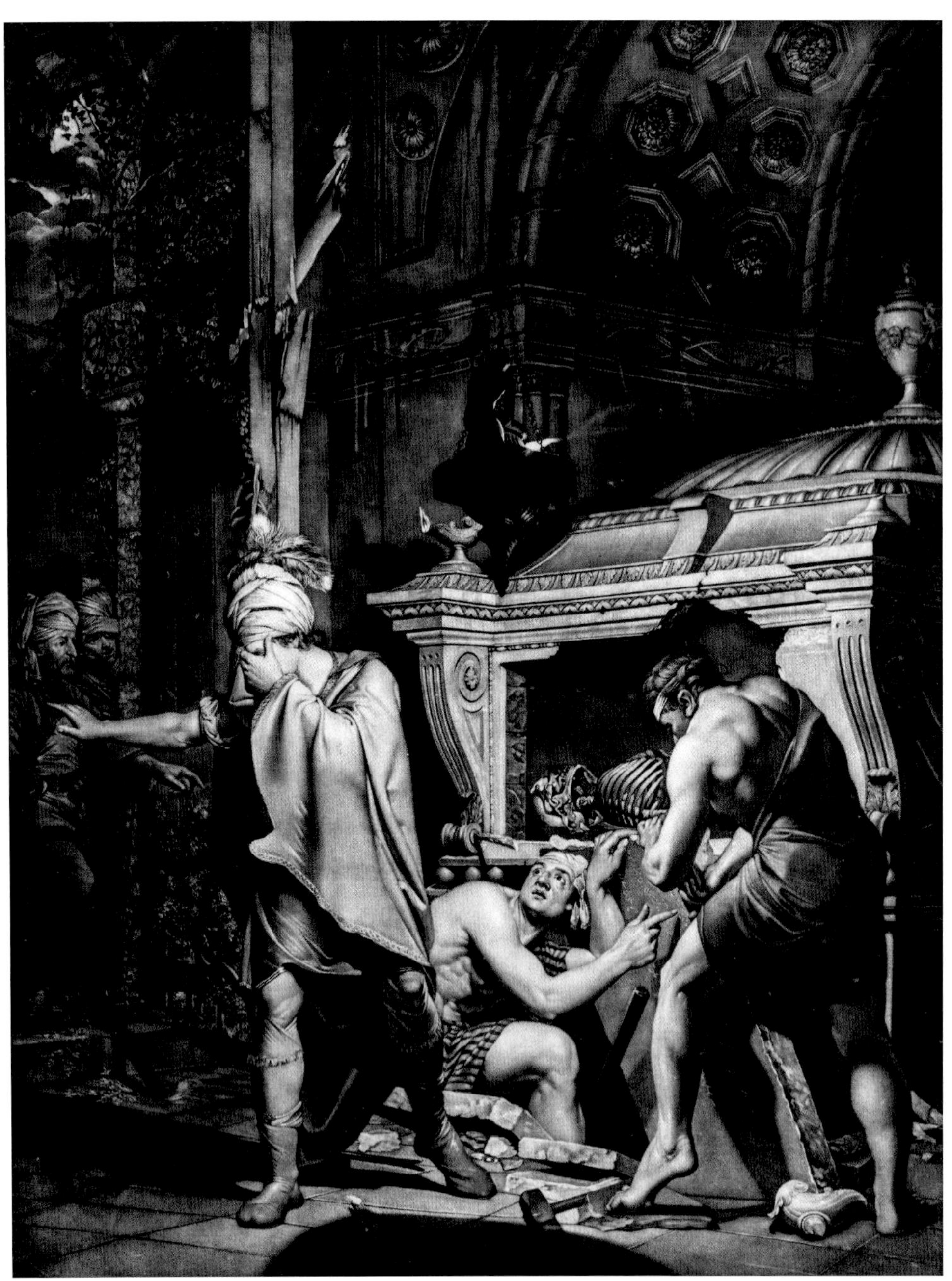

27

Valentine Green after Joseph Wright of Derby
Miravan, 1772
Mezzotint, 51.5 × 36.3 cm
Derby Museums

NOTES

BETWEEN DARKNESS AND LIGHT

Christine Riding

1 *Le pour et le contre* 1767, p. 18.
2 Wright 1995, p. 112. The most recent in-depth discussion of Joseph Wright's art, career and reputation is Craske 2020. For a summary of commentaries on Wright from the post-war period onwards, see 'Introduction' in Craske 2020, pp. 1–7.
3 Robertson 2015, p. 2; Allen 2017, p. 2.
4 London, Paris and New York 1990, p. 10.
5 London, Dublin and Edinburgh 2016–17, pp. 97–112.
6 See Riding and Llewellyn 2013; Duro 2010.
7 Catskill 2018, pp. 20–1, 14–15, 88–91; London 2013–14, pp. 42–3; Riding 2013A, pp. 112, 118–20.
8 Solkin 2015, pp. 125–7, 149–74.
9 Ibid., pp. 148–54.
10 London 2024–5, pp. 13–15.
11 London 2024–5, p. 14; Houston 2007–8, pp. 37–8; Bowson 2016, vii, pp. 265–6.
12 See London 2018, pp. 30–5.
13 Boswell 1791, entry dated 11 April 1776, p. 61. For Hannah Wright's unpublished biography, see Wright 1850.
14 It should be noted here that Caravaggio, now a seminal figure in the history of Western art, was barely mentioned in eighteenth-century British writings or surveys of European art. See Nottingham and London 1998, pp. 9–11; Treves 2016–17, pp. 21–9.
15 Bamford and Wallis 2024, pp. 11–12; London, Paris and New York 1990, pp. 10–11.
16 Craske 2020, p. 12.
17 Ibid., pp. 12–13; Fraser 1990, pp. 15–17.
18 Craske 2020, p. 17; Derby 2025, pp. 14–17.
19 Houston 2007–8, pp. 7–11, 26.
20 Riding 2021, pp. 139–40, 195–6, 224–46; Solkin 2015, pp. 99–104.
21 Solkin 2015, pp. 99–101.
22 London 2017–18, pp. 93–118.
23 Derby 2025, p. 8; Derby 2023, pp. 11–12, 104–6.
24 Derby 2023, pp. 105–6.
25 Liverpool and New Haven 2007–8, p. 13.
26 Solkin 2015, pp. 150–1.
27 The paintings Joseph Wright exhibited at the Society of Artists are listed in Graves 1969 [1907], pp. 286–7.
28 Solkin 2015, p. 151.
29 Ibid., p. 152.
30 New Haven and Cardiff 2014, pp. 128–9; Catskill 2018, p. 90.
31 London 2002–3, pp. 98–9.
32 London 2005, pp. 204–5.
33 Fort Worth, Baltimore and London 2004–5, p. 70.
34 Egerton 1998, pp. 242–4; Fort Worth, Baltimore and London 2004–5, pp. 114–15.
35 Liverpool and New Haven 2007–8, p. 130.
36 London, Paris and New York 1990, p. 61; Craske 2020, pp. 90–6.
37 Hubert Le Sueur, *Borghese Gladiator*, about 1630, RCIN 71436.
38 London 2002, pp. 60–1, illustrated p. 61.
39 London, Paris and New York 1990, p. 50.
40 Nottingham and London 1998, pp. 11–12.
41 See, for example, *The Night School* (before 1665, Rijksmuseum) and *An Astronomer by Candlelight* (about 1665, J. Paul Getty Museum); Washington, London and The Hague 2000–1, pp. 120–1, 126–7.
42 Egerton 1998, p. 335.
43 Ibid., p. 340.
44 Craske 2020, p. 28.
45 See Jones 1990, pp. 267–8.
46 Jones 1990, p. 268; Liverpool and New Haven 2007–8, pp. 66–7; Siemon 2025, p. 250.
47 Signal from silver was particularly evident at the edge of the vessel where overlying paint layers were less blocking of the relevant X-rays than in the illuminated volume of the vessel. Catherine Higgitt and Joshua Hill, unpublished Scientific department report, macro X-ray fluorescence (MA-XRF) scanning, NG725, 17–18 February 2025 (selected areas). Technical research into Wright's use of metal has been carried out by Kari Rayner and Douglas MacLennan, Associate Paintings Conservators at the J. Paul Getty Museum. This will be presented in a forthcoming volume accompanying an exhibition organised by the Getty, opening in December 2026. See Siemon 2025, p. 249, n. 40.
48 Solkin 2003, p. 167; Liverpool and New Haven 2007–8, p. 66.
49 San Francisco, Baltimore and London 1997–8; Munich 2019, pp. 51–63, 114–21; London, Dublin and Edinburgh 2016–17, pp. 13–19.
50 The exhibition dates given here follow those recently proposed in Siemon 2025, p. 257.
51 See Lincoln 2016. 'Pictor noctium' was appended to the portrait of Adam de Coster from the influential print series, *Iconography* (1626) by Anthony van Dyck. See www.britishmuseum.org/collection/object/P_R-1a-85 (accessed 18 August 2025).
52 Siemon 2025, p. 251.
53 Nottingham and London 1998, pp. 5–7.
54 Ibid., p. 5.
55 Ibid., p. 6.
56 https://collections.britishart.yale.edu/catalog/tms:940 (accessed 4 August 2025). The paintings Henry Robert Morland exhibited at the Society of Artists are listed in Graves 1969 [1907], pp. 175–6.
57 *Universal Museum* 1767, p. 168.
58 Genesis 1:3, King James Version.
59 John 8:12, King James Version.
60 Robertson 2015, p. 2. See also Plato 2012, pp. 248–53.
61 The print was first published in 1772, after a design by Charles Nicolas Cochin fils: www.britishmuseum.org/collection/object/P_1873-0510-3612 (accessed 4 August 2025).
62 Robertson 2015, pp. 2, 8.
63 Robertson 2021, pp. 37–41.
64 Ibid., pp. xix–xx, 38, 41; for the development of scientific instruments, see p. 49.
65 London, Paris and New York 1990, pp. 54–5.
66 Egerton 1998, p. 337.
67 Ferguson 1764, p. 119.

68 The orrery made by John Rowley for the Earl of Orrery (1712–13) is in the collection of the Science Museum, London (object no. 1952-73).
69 For orreries of varying scale, complexity and decoration, including 'George II's Grand Orrery', see https://collection.sciencemuseumgroup.org.uk/search/objects/object_type/orrery (accessed 18 August 2025).
70 Craske 2020, pp. 20, 107.
71 London, Paris and New York 1990, p. 58. Ferguson's lectures were first published in 1760. See Ferguson 1764.
72 Robertson 2015, pp. 83–5; Robertson 2021, pp. 357, 364.
73 Uglow 2011, p. 177.
74 *Mr and Mrs Thomas Coltman* may have been the 'small conversation' exhibited at the Society of Artists in 1771. See Egerton 1998, p. 344.
75 Retford 2017, pp. 24–7, 65–6.
76 Harris 1719, pp. 159–82, with an illustration of the grand orrery between pp. 158 and 159; Martin 1755/59, p. 405.
77 Kuretsky 2017.
78 Hoare 2018, pp. 175–6, illustrated p. 174. Although the painting is traditionally described as a self portrait, some scholars have suggested it is a portrait of Rosa's friend Giovan Battista Ricciardi (see p. 175).
79 Betz 2019.
80 Cheyne 1733, p. ii.
81 London, Paris and New York 1990, p. 111.
82 Hoare 2018, pp. 223–5; Craske 2020, pp. 2–4, 28.
83 Solkin 2003, p. 170.
84 Brooks 1999, pp. 110–11.
85 Craske 2020, pp. 172–8.
86 Riding and Llewellyn 2013.
87 See Riding and Llewellyn 2013 for definitions of the sublime during this period. For a discussion of darkness, racism and the sublime, see Thomas 2021–2.
88 Catskill 2018, pp. 99–113.
89 Riding 2021–2.
90 Catskill 2018, pp. 20–1.
91 Mortimer subsequently produced a drawing of the Italian artist seated in a rugged landscape setting that was published as a print and dedicated to Joshua Reynolds. See Hoare 2018, pp. 27–9; the print, entitled 'Salvator Rosa', is illustrated on p. 27.
92 Catskill 2018, pp. 88–9; Craske 2020, pp. 163, 170.
93 Catskill 2018, p. 89.
94 Riding and Llewellyn 2013.
95 Duro 2010, pp. 661–2, 670.
96 Sarafianos 2013.
97 Riding 2013B. Stubbs first exhibited a painting of an exotic animal at the Society of Artists in 1763. The subject was a zebra owned by Queen Charlotte (now in the Yale Center for British Art, accession no. B1981.25.617). See Graves 1907 [1969], p. 249.

A 'PECULIAR' PAINTER OF CANDLELIGHT

Jon King

1 Quoted in Egerton 1998, p. 334. See also Barker 2003.
2 Hayley 1783, p. 9.
3 See 'Peculiar' in Johnson 1755.
4 Quoted in Bamford and Wallis 2024, p. 41.
5 Wright 1850, p. 2.
6 Ibid., pp. 2–3.
7 This porcelain group was purchased by Lady Charlotte Schreiber from a London source in 1881. It served as a model widely imitated by British porcelain factories and is adapted from Charles Nicolas Cochin's engraving *Foire de Campagne*, after a design by François Boucher. Known in factory records as *La Curiosité* and *La Loterie*, the design also inspired reproductions at the Doccia factory in Italy. For a detailed discussion of this model and a listing of public collections in which examples can be found, see Sèvres 2001–2, nos 72 and 73.
8 Paper peepshows developed out of sturdier ones such as the one shown at pl. 15, in which views were slid at regular intervals into a rigid box made of wood or cardboard, with the peephole located at one end. The layered structure of this peepshow was inspired by Baroque stage sets where the décor was painted onto a series of parallel planes that moved along grooves set in the stage. Martin Engelbrecht was a German engraver and publisher.
9 Quoted in Craske 2020, p. 34.
10 Bamford and Wallis 2024, p. 10.
11 Gernsheim and Gernsheim 1955. Gainsborough's showbox can be found in the V&A Collection, P.44:1 to 4-1955.
12 Craske 2020, p. 32.
13 See Stafford 1994, p. 293.
14 Bolla 2003.
15 Monteyne 2013, pp. 201–2; Newton 1704.
16 Craske 2020, p. 32.
17 See Hogarth's etching *Southwark Fair* (1733), which uses the peepshow as a symbol of lowbrow escapism, drawing attention to its role in mesmerising participants and reflecting the chaos and vice of the surrounding environment.
18 Monteyne 2013, pp. 195, 201.
19 Egerton 1998, p. 336.
20 Ibid., p. 335. See also Norwich 1988, p. 8.
21 See Craske 2020, pp. 34–5.
22 Lairesse 1807, p. 210, cited in Craske 2020, p. 35.
23 Bolla 2003, p. 66. Peter de Bolla writes that the 'narrative thrust' of Wright's candlelight paintings draws them 'toward history'.
24 Craske 2020, pp. 89–97.
25 See Chard 1994, pp. 142–55.
26 Solkin 1993, pp. 215–23. See also Ezell 1983, Locke 1689 and Locke 1693.
27 Gandon 1846, p. 211.
28 Craske 2020, p. 111.
29 Quoted in Fraser 1990, p. 18.
30 For more on the concept of the 'scientific sublime' in Wright's work, see Duro 2010.
31 Bamford and Wallis 2024, p. 33.
32 Donald 2007, p. 17.

33 Solkin 1993, p. 235; Smith 1790, pp. 78–9.
34 For more on the conspicuous absence of mothers in Wright's candlelight paintings, see Siddons 2015.
35 Bolla 2003, p. 47. For more on this painting in relation to the history of childhood in eighteenth-century art, see Berkeley, Memphis and Omaha 1995–6, p. 196. For more on this painting in relation to Wright and the history of the air pump, see Craske 2020, p. 125.
36 Bolla 2003, pp. 62–71. De Bolla states that Wright's candlelight paintings from the 1760s 'didactically present an encyclopaedia of looks'.
37 During 2002, pp. 102, 285–6. Originating in Berlin in 1789, the phantasmagoria reached London in 1801 under the management of Paul de Philipsthal, who was a partner of Madame Tussaud. The term 'phantasmagoria' was popularised by Scottish essayist and historian Thomas Carlyle. For more on Ouvrier's print, see Monteyne 2013, fig. 145, p. 206.
38 Quoted and translated in Wolff 1998, p. 378. See also Rousseau 1966 [1762], pp. 133–9.
39 The story of Pygmalion is told in Ovid's *Metamorphoses*, Book X. This is also linked to more lusty depictions by Schalcken in Craske 2020, p. 98.
40 See Hargraves 2005.
41 Bamford and Wallis 2024, p. 30.
42 Solkin 1993, pp. 239–44.
43 Quoted, translated and discussed further in Wolff 1998, p. 387. See also Condillac 1754.
44 Solkin 1993, pp. 239–44.
45 See Higonnet 1998, M. Postle in Bath and Kendal 2005, pp. 7–24, and Langmuir 2006.
46 See Egerton 1998, pp. 92–100.
47 See Schama 1987, pp. 481–561.
48 For more on the painting within the broader context of cat paintings, see Foucart-Walter and Rosenberg 1988, p. 164, and Leach 2017.
49 For instance, see Bryant 1996.
50 See Nottingham and London 1998, pp. 68–70. For an interpretation of the painting in relation to Wright's erotic depictions of women and girls, see Siegfried 1999, pp. 47–9.
51 For a detailed analysis of *The Hermit* and Wright's numerous other depictions of old men and philosophers, see Craske 2020, pp. 137–67.
52 Craske 2020, p. 137. Wright tried to sell *The Hermit* to Empress Catherine the Great of Russia, but she rejected it, instead purchasing *An Iron Forge viewed from Without* (fig. 14).
53 In fact, the mezzotints have often been regarded as such, maintaining their popularity among collectors as distinctive 'masterpieces' in their own right. See Davis 1949 and Clayton 1990, p. 28. For examples of the print connoisseur's sustained interest in mezzotints after Wright from the eighteenth through to the twentieth centuries, see Chelsum 1786, p. 9; Whitman 1898, pp. 36–8; Whitman 1902, pp. 12, 35, 126, 129; Morris 1932; and Buckley 1957.
54 Monteyne 2013, especially chapter six.
55 From the late seventeenth century, the English capital saw the number of major print-sellers rise from just two to over sixty. See Brewer 2013, p. 362, and Clayton 1997.
56 Bamford and Wallis 2024, p. 11. Following one of his frequent disputes with the academicians, Wright expressed this in 1791, stating, 'I consider the exhibition as my Mart', highlighting how vital exhibitions were for reaching his audience.
57 As artist William Gilpin wrote, in the print 'you can more easily trace the principles of light and shade', and while engraving and etching techniques involved demarcating 'the shades', the mezzotint was unique, for the tonal contrast was achieved through working away 'the lights'. See Gilpin 1768, pp. 36, 57.
58 See Morris 1932, p. 95.
59 London, Paris and New York 1990, pp. 234–6, 238–43, 246.
60 For example, in 1885 poet and critic William Cosmo Monkhouse wrote that 'engravings after Wright by Earlom, J.R. Smith, Val. Green, Pether, and others, are still sought after'. See Monkhouse 1885, p. vi.
61 Clayton 1990; Barker 2009, p. 4. It is difficult to know Wright's financial gains from prints as he did not record them in his early account books. The importance of mezzotints to Wright's reputation was first noted by his obituarist, John Leigh Philips. See Philips 1797.
62 Frye's influence on Wright was first discovered by Benedict Nicolson in 1968 and has been discussed frequently in subsequent publications. See Nicolson 1968, pp. 42–4; London, Paris and New York 1990, p. 10; Egerton 1998, p. 335; Clayton 1990, p. 26; and Craske 2020, pp. 100–7.
63 Craske 2020, pp. 100–7. Craske argues that Frye used candlelight and facial expression to turn the static portrait into a narrative painting, as celebrated by literary figures such as Tobias Smollett.
64 Bamford and Wallis 2024, p. 15.

BIBLIOGRAPHY

Allen 2017 R.C. Allen, *The Industrial Revolution: A Very Short Introduction*, Oxford 2017

Bamford and Wallis 2024 L. Bamford and J. Wallis, *Joseph Wright of Derby: An Introduction to his Life and Work through the Collection at Derby Museums*, Derby 2024

Barker 2003 E.E. Barker, '"A very great and uncommon genius in a peculiar way": Joseph Wright of Derby and Candlelight Painting in Eighteenth-Century Britain', PhD dissertation, Institute of Fine Arts, New York 2003

Barker 2009 E.E. Barker, 'Documents Relating to Joseph Wright "of Derby"', *The Volume of the Walpole Society*, 71 (2009), pp. 1–216

Bath and Kendal 2005 M. Postle and A. Wright, *Pictures of Innocence: Portraits of Children from Hogarth to Lawrence*, exh. cat., Holburne Museum of Art, Bath; Abbot Hall Art Gallery, Kendal 2005

Berkeley, Memphis and Omaha 1995–6 J.C. Steward, *The New Child: British Art and the Origins of Modern Childhood, 1730–1830*, exh. cat., University Art Museum, Berkeley, CA 1995; Dixon Gallery and Gardens, Memphis, TN 1995–6; Joslyn Art Museum, Omaha, NE 1996

Betz 2019 E. Betz, 'Melancholy: The Evolution of the English Malady, c. 1550–1750', *Trinity Postgraduate Review Journal*, 18, no. 1 (2019), pp. 95–113

Bolla 2003 P. de Bolla, *The Education of the Eye: Painting, Landscape, and Architecture in Eighteenth-Century Britain*, Stanford, CA 2003

Boswell 1791 J. Boswell, *Life of Samuel Johnson*, vol. 2, London 1791

Bowson 2016 E.P. Bowson, *Pompeo Batoni: A Complete Catalogue of his Paintings*, vol. 1, New Haven, CT, and London 2016

Brewer 2013 J. Brewer, *The Pleasures of the Imagination: English Culture in the Eighteenth Century*, London 2013

Brooks 1999 C. Brooks, *The Gothic Revival*, London 1999

Bryant 1996 J. Bryant, 'The Dark Side of "The Kitten": A Wright of Derby for Kenwood', *Apollo*, 144, no. 418 (1996), pp. 18–19

Buckley 1957 C.E. Buckley, 'Joseph Wright of Derby in Mezzotint', *Antiques*, 72, no. 5 (1957), pp. 440–2

Catskill 2018 T. Barringer et al., *Picturesque and Sublime: Thomas Cole's Trans-Atlantic Inheritance*, exh. cat., Thomas Cole National Historic Site, Catskill, NY 2018

Chard 1994 C. Chard, 'Effeminacy, Pleasure and the Classical Body', in *Femininity and Masculinity in Eighteenth-Century Art and Culture*, ed. G. Perry and M. Rossington, Manchester and New York 1994, pp. 142–61

Chelsum 1786 J. Chelsum, *A History of the Art of Engraving in Mezzotinto, from its Origin to the Present Times, Including an Account of the Works of the Earliest Artists*, Winchester 1786

Cheyne 1733 G. Cheyne, *The English Malady: or, A Treatise of Nervous Diseases of all Kinds*, London 1733

Clayton 1990 T. Clayton, 'The Engraving and Publication of Prints of Joseph Wright's Paintings', in London, Paris and New York 1990, pp. 25–30

Clayton 1997 T. Clayton, *The English Print, 1688–1802*, New Haven, CT 1997

Condillac 1754 E. Bonnot de Condillac, *Traité des sensations*, London and Paris 1754

Craske 2020 M. Craske, *Joseph Wright of Derby: Painter of Darkness*, New Haven, CT 2020

Davis 1949 F. Davis, 'A Page for Collectors. Eighteenth-Century Sentiment and Science', *Illustrated London News*, 29 October 1949, p. 674

Derby 2023 J. Riding, *Hogarth's Britons*, exh. cat., Derby Museum and Art Gallery, Derby 2023

Derby 2025 L. Bamford, *Joseph Wright of Derby: Life on Paper*, exh. cat., Derby Museum and Art Gallery, Derby 2025

Donald 2007 D. Donald, *Picturing Animals in Britain*, London and New Haven, CT 2007

During 2002 S. During, *Modern Enchantments: The Cultural Power of Secular Magic*, Cambridge, MA 2002

Duro 2010 P. Duro, '"Great and Noble Ideas of the Moral Kind": Wright of Derby and the Scientific Sublime', *Art History*, 33, no. 4 (2010), pp. 660–79

Egerton 1998 J. Egerton, *The British School*, National Gallery Catalogues, London 1998

Ezell 1983 M.J.M. Ezell, 'John Locke's Images of Childhood: Early Eighteenth-Century Response to "Some Thoughts Concerning Education"', *Eighteenth-Century Studies*, 17, no. 2 (1983), pp. 139–55

Ferguson 1764 J. Ferguson, *Lectures on Select Subjects*, London 1764

Fort Worth, Baltimore and London 2004–5 M. Warner, *Stubbs and the Horse*, exh. cat., Kimbell Art Museum, Fort Worth, TX 2004–5; The Walters Art Museum, Baltimore, MD 2005; The National Gallery, London 2005

Foucart-Walter and Rosenberg 1988 E. Foucart-Walter and P. Rosenberg, *The Painted Cat: The Cat in Western Painting from the Fifteenth to the Twentieth Century*, New York 1988

Fraser 1990 D. Fraser, 'Joseph Wright of Derby and the Lunar Society', in London, Paris and New York 1990, pp. 15–23

Gandon 1846 J. Gandon, *The Life of James Gandon, Esq.*, ed. J. Gandon [Jr] and T.J. Mulvany, Dublin 1846

Gernsheim and Gernsheim 1955 H. Gernsheim, in collaboration with A. Gernsheim, *The History of Photography from the Earliest Use of the Camera Obscura in the Eleventh Century up to 1914*, London 1955

Gilpin 1768 W. Gilpin, *An Essay Upon Prints*, London 1768

Graves 1969 [1907] A. Graves, *The Society of Artists of Great Britain (1760–1791) and The Free Society of Artists (1761–1783)*, Bath 1969 [1907]

Hargraves 2005 M. Hargraves, *Candidates for Fame: The Society of Artists of Great Britain, 1760–1791*, London and New Haven, CT 2005

Harris 1719 J. Harris, *Astronomical Dialogues between a Gentleman and a Lady*, London 1719

Hayley 1783 W. Hayley, *Ode to Mr. Wright of Derby*, Chichester 1783

Higonnet 1998 A. Higonnet, *Pictures of Innocence: The History and Crisis of Ideal Childhood*, London 1998

Hoare 2018 A. Hoare, *Salvator Rosa, Friendship and the Free Artist in Seventeenth-Century Italy*, Studies in Baroque Art, vol. 9, Turnhout 2018

Houston 2007–8 E.P. Bowron and P.B. Kerber, *Pompeo Batoni: Prince of Painters in Eighteenth-Century Rome*, exh. cat., Museum of Fine Arts, Houston, TX 2007–8

Johnson 1755 S. Johnson, *A Dictionary of the English Language*, vol. 2, 1st folio edn, London 1755

Jones 1990 R. Jones, 'Wright of Derby's Techniques of Painting', in London, Paris and New York 1990, pp. 263–71

Kuretsky 2017 S. Donahue Kuretsky, 'Light and Sight in ter Brugghen's *Man Writing by Candlelight*', *Journal of Historians of Netherlandish Art*, 9, no. 1 (2017), DOI: 10.5092/jhna.2017.9.1.4 (accessed 18 August 2025)

Lairesse 1807 G. de Lairesse, *A Treatise on the Art of Painting*, vol. 1, London 1807

Langmuir 2006 E. Langmuir, *Imagining Childhood*, New Haven, CT, and London 2006

***Le pour et le contre* 1767** *Le pour et le contre: Being a Poetical Display of the Merit and Demerit of the Capital Paintings Exhibited at Spring Gardens*, London 1767

Leach 2017 S. Leach, 'Miss Kitty: "Two girls decorating a cat by candlelight" by Joseph Wright of Derby (1734–1797)', *The British Art Journal*, 17, no. 3 (2017), pp. 44–6

Lincoln 2016 M.D. Lincoln, 'Sources for Gerrit van Honthorst's Italian Nickname', *Notes in the History of Art*, 35, no. 3 (2016), pp. 244–9

Liverpool and New Haven 2007–8 E.E. Barker and A. Kidson (eds), *Joseph Wright of Derby in Liverpool*, exh. cat., Walker Art Gallery, Liverpool 2007–8; Yale Center for British Art, New Haven, CT 2008

Llewellyn and Riding 2013 N. Llewellyn and C. Riding (eds), *The Art of the Sublime*, ed. Tate Research Publication, January 2013: www.tate.org.uk/art/research-publications/the-sublime/christine-riding-and-nigel-llewellyn-british-art-and-the-sublime-r1109418 (accessed 4 August 2025)

Locke 1689 J. Locke, *An Essay Concerning Human Understanding*, London 1689

Locke 1693 J. Locke, *Some Thoughts Concerning Education*, London 1693

London 2002 A. Kidson, *George Romney 1734–1802*, exh. cat., National Portrait Gallery, London 2002

London 2002–3 M. Rosenthal and M. Myrone, *Gainsborough*, exh. cat., Tate Britain, London 2002–3

London 2005 M. Postle (ed.), *Joshua Reynolds: The Creation of Celebrity*, exh. cat., Tate Britain, London 2005

London 2013–14 C. Riding and R. Johns, *Turner & the Sea*, exh. cat., National Maritime Museum, London 2013–14

London 2017–18 J. Riding, *Basic Instincts: Love, Passion and Violence in the Art of Joseph Highmore*, exh. cat., Foundling Museum, London 2017–18

London 2018 J. Wood, 'Artists and Agents: Connoisseurship at the Caroline Court', in *Charles I: King and Collector*, ed. P. Rumberg and D. Shawe-Taylor, exh. cat., Royal Academy of Arts in partnership with Royal Collection Trust, London 2018, pp. 30–5

London 2021–2 C. Riding (ed.), *Kehinde Wiley: The Prelude*, exh. cat., The National Gallery, London 2021–2

London 2024–5 C. Riding, 'Introduction: Nature and Nation', in *Discover Constable & The Hay Wain*, ed. C. Riding, exh. cat., The National Gallery, London 2024–5, pp. 10–25

London, Dublin and Edinburgh 2016–17 L. Treves, *Beyond Caravaggio*, exh. cat., The National Gallery, London 2016–17; National Gallery of Ireland, Dublin 2017; Royal Scottish Academy, Edinburgh 2017

London, Paris and New York 1990 J. Egerton, *Wright of Derby*, exh. cat., Tate, London; Grand Palais, Paris; The Metropolitan Museum of Art, New York 1990

Martin 1755/9 B. Martin, *The Young Gentleman and Lady's Philosophy ... By Way of a Dialogue*, vol. 1 'The Philosophy of the Heavens and of the Atmosphere', London 1755/9

Monkhouse 1885 W.C. Monkhouse, 'Preface', in W. Bemrose, *The Life and Works of Joseph Wright, A.R.A., Commonly Called 'Wright of Derby'*, London 1885, pp. v–vii

Monteyne 2013 J. Monteyne, *From Still Life to the Screen: Print Culture, Display, and the Materiality of the Image in Eighteenth-Century London*, New Haven, CT 2013

Morris 1932 R. Morris, 'Engravings after Joseph Wright A.R.A.', *The Print Collector's Quarterly*, 19 (1932), pp. 94–115

Munich 2019 B. Ebert and L.M. Helmus, *Utrecht, Caravaggio and Europe*, exh. cat., Alte Pinakothek, Munich 2019

New Haven and Cardiff 2014 M. Postle, 'Inspiration and Imitation: Wilson, London, and "The School of Rome"', in *Richard Wilson and the Transformation of European Landscape Painting*, ed. M. Postle and R. Simon, exh. cat., Yale Center for British Art, New Haven, CT; National Museum Cardiff 2014, pp. 119–47

Newton 1704 I. Newton, *Opticks*, London 1704

Nicolson 1968 B. Nicolson, *Joseph Wright of Derby: Painter of Light*, London 1968

Norwich 1988 A.W. Moore, *Dutch and Flemish Painting in Norfolk: A History of Taste and Influence, Fashion and Collecting*, exh. cat., Norwich Castle Museum / Norfolk Museums Service, Norwich 1988

Nottingham and London 1998 M. Postle, *Angels and Urchins: The Fancy Picture in Eighteenth-Century British Art*, exh. cat., Djanogly Art Gallery, Nottingham; Kenwood House, London 1998

Philips 1797 J.L. Philips, 'Memoirs of the Life and Principal Works of the Late Joseph Wright of Derby', *Monthly Magazine*, October 1797, pp. 289–94

Plato 2012 Plato, *The Republic*, trans. Christopher Rowe, London 2012

Retford 2017 K. Retford, *The Conversation Piece: Making Modern Art in Eighteenth-Century Britain*, New Haven, CT, and London 2017

Riding 2013A C. Riding, 'Shipwreck in French and British Visual Art, 1700–1842: Vernet, Northcote, Géricault, and Turner', in *Shipwreck in Art and Literature: Images and Interpretations from Antiquity to the Present Day*, ed. C. Thompson, New York and Abingdon 2013, pp. 112–32

Riding 2013B C. Riding, 'Shipwreck, Self-Preservation and the Sublime', in Llewellyn and Riding 2013

Riding 2021 J. Riding, *Hogarth: Life in Progress*, London 2021

Riding 2021–2 C. Riding, 'The Nature of Our Looking', in London 2021–2, p. 44

Riding and Llewellyn 2013 C. Riding and N. Llewellyn, 'British Art and the Sublime', in Llewellyn and Riding 2013

Robertson 2015 J. Robertson, *The Enlightenment: A Very Short Introduction*, Oxford 2015

Robertson 2021 R. Robertson, *The Enlightenment: The Pursuit of Happiness, 1680–1790*, London 2021

Rousseau 1966 [1762] J.-J. Rousseau, *Emile, ou de l'éducation*, ed. M. Launay, Paris 1966 [1762]

San Francisco, Baltimore and London 1997–8 W. Franits, 'Emerging from the Shadows: Genre Painting by the Utrecht Caravaggisti and its Contemporary Reception', in *Masters of Light: Dutch Painters in Utrecht during the Golden Age*, ed. J.A. Spicer with L. Federle Orr, exh. cat., Fine Arts Museums of San Francisco, CA 1997; The Walters Art Gallery, Baltimore, MD 1998; The National Gallery, London 1998, pp. 114–20

Sarafianos 2013 A. Sarafianos, 'Sublime Action: George Stubbs's Lion and Horse series', in Llewellyn and Riding 2013

Schama 1987 S. Schama, *The Embarrassment of Riches: An Interpretation of Dutch Culture in the Golden Age*, London 1987

Sèvres 2001–2 *Falconet à Sèvres 1757–1766, ou l'art de plaire*, with texts by A. Faÿ-Hallé et al., exh. cat., Musée national de céramique, Sèvres 2001–2

Siddons 2015 L. Siddons, 'Sensibility and Science: Motherhood and the Gendering of Knowledge in Two Mezzotints after Joseph Wright of Derby', *A Journal of Women's Studies*, 36, no. 2 (2015), pp. 124–51

Siegfried 1999 S.L. Siegfried, 'Engaging the Audience: Sexual Economies of Vision in Joseph Wright', *Representations*, 68 (1999), pp. 34–58

Siemon 2025 J. Siemon, '"Two Boys with a Bladder" in the J. Paul Getty Museum and Joseph Wright of Derby's Early Candlelights', *The Burlington Magazine*, 167, no. 1464 (2025), pp. 242–57

Smith 1790 A. Smith, *The Theory of Moral Sentiments*, vol. 2, 6th edn, London and Edinburgh 1790

Solkin 1993 D.H. Solkin, *Painting for Money: The Visual Arts and the Public Sphere in Eighteenth-Century England*, London and New Haven, CT 1993

Solkin 2003 D.H. Solkin, 'Joseph Wright of Derby and the Sublime Art of Labor', *Representations*, 83, no. 1 (2003), pp. 167–94

Solkin 2015 D.H. Solkin, *Art in Britain 1660–1815*, Pelican History of Art, New Haven, CT 2015

Stafford 1994 B.M. Stafford, *Artful Science: Enlightenment Entertainment and the Eclipse of Visual Education*, Cambridge, MA 1994

Thomas 2021–2 S. Thomas, 'The Dark Side of the Landscape', in London 2021–2, pp. 65–75

Treves 2016–17 L. Treves, 'Caravaggio and Britain: Early Appreciation, Later Criticism and Missed Opportunities', in London, Dublin and Edinburgh 2016–17

Uglow 2011 J. Uglow, *The Lunar Men: The Friends who Made the Future, 1730–1810*, London 2011

***Universal Museum* 1767** 'Strictures on the Present Exhibition of Paintings at Spring Gardens', *The Universal Museum and Complete Magazine of Knowledge and Pleasure for April 1767*

Washington, London and The Hague 2000–1 A.K. Wheelock, Jr (ed.), *Gerrit Dou 1613–1675: Master Painter in the Age of Rembrandt*, exh. cat., National Gallery of Art, Washington, DC 2000; Dulwich Picture Gallery, London 2000; Royal Cabinet of Paintings Mauritshuis, The Hague 2000–1

Whitman 1898 A. Whitman, *The Masters of Mezzotint: The Men and their Work*, London 1898

Whitman 1902 A. Whitman, *Valentine Green*, London 1902

Wolff 1998 L. Wolff, 'When I Imagine a Child: The Idea of Childhood and the Philosophy of Memory in the Enlightenment', *Eighteenth-Century Studies*, 31, no. 4 (1998), pp. 377–401

Wright 1850 H. Wright, 'Memoir', 1850, Derby Local Studies Library, Derby, MS 11172

Wright 1995 C. Wright, *The Masters of Candlelight*, Landshut 1995

EXHIBITED WORKS

Works are listed chronologically under each artist. Unless otherwise stated, the works are exhibited in London and Derby.

Pl. 4 Lorenzo Bartolini (1777–1850) after Antoine Coysevox (1640–1720), *Nymph with a Shell*, 1822, Carrara marble, 34 × 39 × 39 cm, Trustees of the Weston Park Foundation

Hendrick ter Brugghen (1588–1629), *The Concert*, about 1626, oil on canvas, 99.1 × 116.8 cm, The National Gallery, London. Bought with contributions from the National Heritage Memorial Fund, the Art Fund and The Pilgrim Trust, 1983 [Derby only, not illustrated]

Pl. 7 Attributed to Benjamin Cole (1695–1766), *Grand Orrery*, about 1750, mahogany, brass, steel, ivory and ebony, 63.5 × 76.2 cm, Dumfries House, part of The King's Foundation [London only]

Pl. 23 Richard Earlom (1743–1822) after Joseph Wright of Derby, *A Blacksmith's Shop*, 1771, mezzotint, 57.4 × 43.2 cm, Derby Museums. Gift of the Reverend Edward Lloyd Simpson, 1939

Pl. 24 Richard Earlom (1743–1822) after Joseph Wright of Derby, *An Iron Forge*, 1773, mezzotint, 47.8 × 59.2 cm, Derby Museums. Transferred from the Bemrose Library to Derby Museums, 1921

Pl. 15 Martin Engelbrecht (1684–1756), *Peepshow, Toy Theatre*, 1721 (probably), wood and engraved paper, 51.5 × 71 × 17 cm, Young V&A. Given by Mr. G.A. Wassermann

Pl. 16 Étienne-Maurice Falconet (1716–1791), *La Lanterne Magique*, about 1757, biscuit porcelain, Sèvres porcelain factory, 15.6 × 16.5 cm, Victoria and Albert Museum. Given by Lady Charlotte Schreiber

Pl. 20 Valentine Green (1739–1813) after Joseph Wright of Derby, *A Philosopher shewing an Experiment on the Air Pump*, 1769, mezzotint, 46.1 × 58.3 cm, Derby Museums. Gift of Hon. Brigadier General William Wright Bemrose, 1912

Pl. 27 Valentine Green (1739–1813) after Joseph Wright of Derby, *Miravan*, 1772, mezzotint, 51.5 × 36.3 cm, Derby Museums. Purchased in 1920

Pl. 8 Nairne & Blunt, *Air Pump (Vacuum Fountain)*, about 1774–93, glass, metal (brass), wood and ivory, 133 × 40.8 × 66 cm, on loan from the Whipple Museum of the History of Science, University of Cambridge

Pl. 19 William Pether (1739–1821) after Joseph Wright of Derby, *A Philosopher giving a Lecture on the Orrery*, 1768, mezzotint, 52 × 64.8 cm, Derby Museums. The H. Cheney Bemrose Bequest, 1954

Pl. 17 William Pether (1739–1821) after Joseph Wright of Derby, *Three Persons viewing the Gladiator by Candlelight*, 1769, mezzotint, 47 × 57 cm, Derby Museums. Gift of the Reverend Edward Lloyd Simpson, 1939

Pl. 25 William Pether (1739–1821) after Joseph Wright of Derby, *An Hermit*, 1770, mezzotint, 60.5 × 48 cm, Derby Museums. Purchased from Robert Ward & Son of Derby, 1923

Pl. 18 William Pether (1739–1821) after Joseph Wright of Derby, *An Academy by Lamplight*, 1771, mezzotint, 58.9 × 46.4 cm, Derby Museums. Gift of the Reverend Edward Lloyd Simpson, 1939

Pl. 22 William Pether (1739–1821) after Joseph Wright of Derby, *A Farrier's Shop*, 1771, mezzotint, 53.2 × 38.3 cm, Derby Museums. The H. Cheney Bemrose Bequest, 1954

Pl. 26 William Pether (1739–1821) after Joseph Wright of Derby, *An Alchymist*, 1775, mezzotint, 62.5 × 50 cm, Derby Museums. Gift of the Bemrose Library, 1924

Godfried Schalcken (1643–1706), *A Candlelight Scene: A Man offering a Gold Chain and Coins to a Girl seated on a Bed*, about 1665–70, oil on copper, 15.5 × 18.9 cm, The National Gallery, London. Wynn Ellis Bequest, 1876 [Derby only, not illustrated]

Pl. 3 Unknown, *Borghese Gladiator*, about 1775–about 1899, bronze, 51 × 38 cm, National Trust Collections, Shugborough (The Anson Collection [accepted in lieu of tax by H.M. Government and transferred to the National Trust in 1966])

Pl. 21 Thomas Watson (1750–1781) after Joseph Wright of Derby, *Miss Kitty dressing*, 1781, mezzotint, 48.6 × 36.5 cm, Derby Museums. Gift of the Reverend Edward Lloyd Simpson, 1939

JOSEPH WRIGHT OF DERBY (1734–1797)

Pl. 1 *Three Persons viewing the Gladiator by Candlelight*, 1765, oil on canvas, 102.5 × 122 cm, Private collection

Pl. 5 *A Philosopher giving that Lecture on the Orrery in which a Lamp is put in the Place of the Sun*, exhibited 1766, oil on canvas, 147.3 × 203.2 cm, Derby Museums. Purchased by public subscription and presented to Derby Museums in 1884

Pl. 9 *A Girl reading a Letter with an Old Man reading over her Shoulder*, about 1767–70, oil on canvas, 91.5 × 71.2 cm, Private collection, c/o Omnia Art

Fig. 1 *Self Portrait in a Black Feathered Hat*, about 1770–3, pastel on blue paper, 53.3 × 36.8 cm, Derby Museums. Purchased with the assistance of the Art Fund, 1953

Pl. 10 *Two Boys fighting over a Bladder*, about 1767–70, oil on canvas, 91.5 × 71.2 cm, Private collection, c/o Omnia Art

Pl. 6 *An Experiment on a Bird in the Air Pump*, 1768, oil on canvas, 183 × 244 cm, The National Gallery, London. Presented by Edward Tyrrell, 1863

Pl. 2 *An Academy by Lamplight*, 1769, oil on canvas, 127 × 101 cm, Yale Center for British Art, Paul Mellon Collection [London only]

Pl. 11 *A Philosopher by Lamplight*, about 1769, oil on canvas, 128.2 × 101.6 cm, Derby Museums. Bequeathed to Derby Museums by Colonel J.G. Burton Borough, 1961

Pl. 12 *The Alchymist in Search of the Philosopher's Stone, discovers Phosphorus, and prays for the Successful Conclusion of his Operation, as was the Custom of the Ancient Chymical Astrologers*, exhibited 1771, reworked and dated 1795, oil on canvas, 127 × 101.6 cm, Derby Museums. Purchased by public subscription and presented to Derby Museums in 1883

Pl. 13 *A Blacksmith's Shop*, 1771, oil on canvas, 125.7 × 99 cm, Derby Museums. Purchased with assistance from the Art Fund, the V&A Purchase Grant Fund, the Pilgrim Trust, and the Friends of Derby Museums, in 1979

Pl. 14 *An Earthstopper on the Banks of the Derwent*, 1773, oil on canvas, 96.5 × 120.6 cm, Derby Museums. Purchased with the assistance of the Art Fund, 1956

ILLUSTRATIONS

Fig. 2 Pompeo Girolamo Batoni (1708–1787), *Portrait of Sir Wyndham Knatchbull-Wyndham*, about 1758, oil on canvas, 233.1 × 161.3 cm, Los Angeles County Museum of Art. Gift of The Ahmanson Foundation (AC1994.128.1)

Fig. 3 *Portrait of Peter Perez Burdett and his First Wife Hannah*, 1765, oil on canvas, 145 × 205 cm, National Gallery, Prague

Fig. 4 William Hogarth (1697–1764), *The March of the Guards to Finchley*, 1750, oil on canvas, 100.3 × 133.3 cm, Foundling Museum, London. Won by the Foundling Hospital in a lottery organised by the artist. Purchased for the Foundling Museum by the National Heritage Memorial Fund with a supporting contribution from the Art Fund, 2005

Fig. 5 Joshua Reynolds (1723–1792), *Garrick between Tragedy and Comedy*, 1761, oil on canvas, 183 × 147.6 cm, Waddesdon Manor

Fig. 6 George Stubbs (1724–1806), *Horse devoured by a Lion*, exhibited 1763, oil on canvas, 69.2 × 103.5 cm, Tate, London. Purchased 1976

Fig. 7 George Romney (1734–1802), *A Conversation (The Artist's Brothers Peter and James Romney)*, 1766, oil on canvas, 110.5 × 87.6 cm, Yale Center for British Art, Paul Mellon Collection

Fig. 8 Gerrit van Honthorst (1592–1656), *The Denial of Saint Peter*, about 1623, oil on canvas, 110.5 × 144.8 cm, Minneapolis Institute of Art. The Putnam Dana McMillan Fund

Fig. 9 Adam de Coster (about 1586–1643), *A Man singing by Candlelight*, between 1625 and 1635, oil on canvas, 123.6 × 90.7 cm, National Gallery of Ireland, Dublin. Purchased 1938

Fig. 10 *Two Boys with a Bladder*, 1767, oil on canvas, 92.7 × 73 cm, J. Paul Getty Museum, Los Angeles

Fig. 11 Jean-Siméon Chardin (1699–1779), *The Young Schoolmistress*, about 1737, oil on canvas, 61.6 × 66.7 cm, The National Gallery, London. Bequeathed by Mrs Edith Cragg, as part of the John Webb Bequest, 1925

Fig. 12 *Mr and Mrs Thomas Coltman*, about 1770–2, oil on canvas, 127 × 101.6 cm, The National Gallery, London. Bought with contributions from the National Heritage Memorial Fund and The Pilgrim Trust, 1984

Fig. 13 Salvator Rosa (1615–1673), *Self Portrait*, about 1647, oil on canvas, 99.1 × 79.4 cm, The Metropolitan Museum of Art, New York. Bequest of Mary L. Harrison, 1921

Fig. 14 *An Iron Forge viewed from Without*, 1773, oil on canvas, 105 × 140 cm, The State Hermitage Museum, St Petersburg

Fig. 15 Richard Wilson (1713/14–1782), *The Destruction of the Children of Niobe*, 1760, oil on canvas, 147.3 × 188 cm, Yale Center for British Art, Paul Mellon Collection

Fig. 16 Charles Amédée Philippe Van Loo (1719–1795), *The Camera Obscura*, 1764, oil on canvas, 88.6 × 88.5 cm, National Gallery of Art, Washington, DC. Gift of Mrs. Robert W. Schuette

Fig. 17 Paul Sandby (1731–1809), *The Cries of London – The Magic Lantern Man*, 1760, etching, 22.2 × 16.1 cm, Philadelphia Museum of Art, Pennsylvania. The Muriel and Philip Berman Gift, acquired from the John S. Phillips bequest of 1876 to the Pennsylvania Academy of the Fine Arts, with funds contributed by Muriel and Philip Berman, gifts (by exchange) of Lisa Norris Elkins, Bryant W. Langston, Samuel S. White 3rd and Vera White, with additional funds contributed by John Howard McFadden, Jr., Thomas Skelton Harrison, and the Philip H. and A.S.W. Rosenbach Foundation, 1985

Fig. 18 Paul Sandby (1731–1809), *Satire with Hogarth as a Magic Lantern projecting a Parody of his 'Paul before Felix'*, 1753, etching, 17.5 × 23 cm, Harvard Art Museums/Fogg Museum, Gift of Marjorie B. Cohn in honor of Richard Balzer, 2008

Fig. 19 Godfried Schalcken (1643–1706), *Young Man and Woman studying a Statue of Venus, by Lamplight*, about 1688–92, oil on canvas, 43.8 × 34.9 cm, The Leiden Collection

Fig. 20 Philippe Joseph Tassaert (1736–1803), *A Drawing Academy*, 1764, pen and brown ink with brown wash over graphite on paper, 33 × 40.6 cm, The British Museum, London

Fig. 21 Study for *An Experiment on a Bird in the Air Pump* (verso of *Self Portrait at the Age of About Forty*), about 1767, oil on canvas, 63.5 × 76.2 cm, Derby Museums. Accepted in lieu of Inheritance Tax by HM Government under a hybrid arrangement and allocated to Derby Museums, administered by Arts Council England, with additional support from the National Heritage Memorial Fund, Art Fund, Robert M. Kirkland DL and a number of private donors and foundations, 2022

Fig. 22 William Pether (1739–1821) after Godfried Schalcken (1643–1706), *Studious Society*, about 1760–80, mezzotint, 30.4 × 25 cm, private collection via Sulis Fine Art

Fig. 23 Arthur Devis (1712–1787), *The John Bacon Family*, between 1742 and 1743, oil on canvas, 76.2 × 131.1 cm, Yale Center for British Art, Paul Mellon Collection

Fig. 24 Jean Ouvrier (1725–1784) after Johann Eleazar Schenau (1737–1806), *La Lanterne Magique*, 1755–84, engraving, 48.4 × 34.9 cm, Yale University Art Gallery, New Haven, CT. Everett V. Meeks, B.A. 1901, Fund

Fig. 25 *An Academy by Lamplight*, 1769, oil on canvas, 127 × 101.6 cm, private collection

Fig. 26 Judith Leyster (1609–1660), *A Boy and a Girl with a Cat and an Eel*, about 1635, oil on wood, 59.4 × 48.8 cm, The National Gallery, London. Bequeathed by C.F. Leach, 1943

Fig. 27 *Two Girls dressing a Kitten by Candlelight*, about 1768–70, oil on canvas, 89 × 69 cm, Kenwood House, The Iveagh Bequest, English Heritage, London

Fig. 28 Salvator Rosa (1615–1673), *Democritus in Meditation*, 1662, etching with drypoint, 46.8 × 28.2 cm, The Metropolitan Museum of Art, New York. Bequest of Phyllis Massar, 2011

Fig. 29 Thomas Frye (about 1710–1762), *Man wearing Cloak*, 1760, mezzotint, 50 × 35 cm, Rijksmuseum, Amsterdam

Fig. 30 Giovanni Cattini (about 1715–about 1800) after Giovanni Battista Piazzetta (1682–1754), *A Young Man leaning on a Staff looking Outward*, 1743, etching, 50.5 × 39.4 cm, The Metropolitan Museum of Art, New York. Gift of Eric W. and Madeleine C. Sorensen, 1994

LIST OF LENDERS

Derby Museums

Dumfries House, part of The King's Foundation

The National Gallery, London

National Trust Collections, Shugborough

Private collection, c/o Omnia Art

Victoria and Albert Museum

Trustees of the Weston Park Foundation

Whipple Museum of the History of Science, University of Cambridge

Yale Center for British Art, Paul Mellon Collection

Young V&A

And those lenders who wish to remain anonymous

ACKNOWLEDGEMENTS

In addition to the comments made in the Directors' Foreword, the curators would like to thank:

Diana Adell, Flora Allen, Annabel Bai Jackson, Spencer Bailey, Lizzie Ballantyne, John Booth, Suzanne Bosman, Davina Cheung, Lady Annie Chichester, John Chu, Jen Cuadrado, Sonia D'Orsi, Janine Derbyshire, Lara Dingemans, Martina Droth, Matt Edwards, Neil Evans, Julie Firth, Davide Gasparotto, Melissa Gustin, Edward and Alison Hicklin, Catherine Higgitt, Joshua Hill, Richard Johns, Hannah Kašpar, Satinder Kaur, Jon King, Jane Knowles, Laura Lappin, Dame Ann Limb, Mary McMahon, Joshua Nall, Gordon Neil, Phoebe Newman, Hannah Payne, Laura Phillips, Anish Rai, Jacqueline Riding, Per Rumberg, Lucy Rutherford, Alice Rylance-Watson, Minnie Scott, Julia Siemon, Simon Spier, Rick Tailby, Holly Tatham, Lucy Wagstaff, Gareth Williams, Jenny Wilson and Esmee Wright

PHOTOGRAPHIC CREDITS

Published to accompany the exhibition

Wright of Derby: From the Shadows
The National Gallery, London: 7 November 2025–10 May 2026
Derby Museum and Art Gallery: 12 June–1 November 2026

Exhibition curated by Christine Riding in London
and Lucy Bamford in Derby

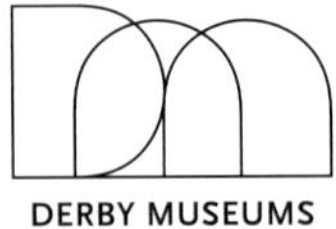

Exhibition supported by

The Thompson Family Charitable Trust

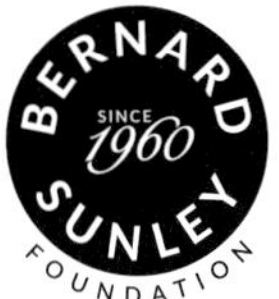

The Sunley Room exhibition programme is supported by the Bernard Sunley Foundation

This exhibition has been made possible by the provision of insurance through the Government Indemnity Scheme. The National Gallery would like to thank HM Government for providing Government Indemnity and the Department for Culture, Media and Sport and Arts Council England for arranging the indemnity.

Authorised Representative in the EU Details:
Easy Access System Europe, Mustamäe tee 50, 10621 Tallinn, Estonia
gpsr.requests@easproject.com

First published in 2025 by
National Gallery Global Limited
Trafalgar Square
London WC2N 5DN
shop.nationalgallery.org.uk

Reprinted 2026

ISBN: 978 1 857097467
1057183

British Library Cataloguing-in-Publication Data
A catalogue record is available from the British Library

Publisher: Laura Lappin
Senior Project Editor: Flora Allen
Copy-editor: Jenny Wilson
Picture Researcher: Suzanne Bosman
Production: Davina Cheung

Designed by Lizzie Ballantyne
Origination by ALTA, London
Printed in London by Park Communications

All works are by Joseph Wright of Derby (1734–1797) unless otherwise stated.
All measurements give height before width.

Cover and page 35: *An Experiment on a Bird in the Air Pump* (details from pl. 6)
Page 2: *A Philosopher by Lamplight* (detail from pl. 11)
Pages 4–5: *Three Persons viewing the Gladiator by Candlelight* (detail from pl. 1)
Page 7: *Two Boys fighting over a Bladder* (detail from pl. 10)
Page 9: *A Blacksmith's Shop* (detail from pl. 13)
Pages 58–9: *A Philosopher giving that Lecture on the Orrery in which a Lamp is put in the Place of the Sun* (detail from pl. 5)

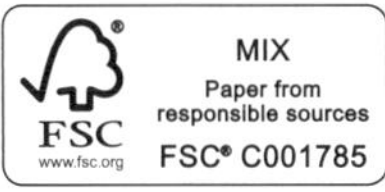